Research in Japanese Sources: A Guide

Research in Japanese Sources:
A Guide

HERSCHEL WEBB

with the assistance of Marleigh Ryan

Published for the East Asian Institute, Columbia University, by

Columbia University Press   *New York and London 1965*

This work was written pursuant to a contract between the United States Office of Education and Columbia University, and is published with the permission of the United States Office of Education, Department of Health, Education, and Welfare.

Copyright © 1963 Columbia University Press
First published in book form 1965
Library of Congress Catalog Card Number: 64–21202
Manufactured in the United States of America

To Ryusaku Tsunoda

Preface

THIS BOOK is intended as a beginner's guide to the subject
of Japanese bibliography. It is designed for three kinds of
users: (1) the student in some discipline of the humanities or
social sciences who wishes to conduct research on Japan and
make use of Japanese-language materials; (2) the student or
librarian who knows no Japanese but wishes information about
Japan; and (3) the student in any discipline whose special
interest may have nothing in particular to do with Japan but
who wishes to consult the work done in his field by Japanese
scholars.

In general I have assumed that readers are familiar with
accepted techniques of scholarly reporting and that they are
trained in the discipline appropriate to their field of study.
I have therefore attempted to exclude matters of bibliography
or reference techniques that pertain solely to one specialized
field. Accordingly, the information on such subjects as statistics,
historiography, and law is limited to what would be useful to
students of the humanities or social sciences in general.

I have made no attempt to list or cite exhaustively the vast
quantity of useful reference books which Japanese scholarship
has produced. My decision to limit severely the number of
individual titles mentioned was based on the conviction that
many of the best and most useful reference works available now
will someday be made obsolete by more up-to-date successors.
The individual works that I do cite by title fall into two main

classes: those few monuments of scholarship whose unique
qualities make it unlikely that they will soon be replaced, and
other works of merit chosen to represent more numerous
classes. I grant that in a sense any guide to a field of scholarly
endeavor will be as ephemeral as progress in the exploration
of the field is rapid. Nevertheless, I believe that the kinds of
reference works that exist and the best techniques for making
use of them have sufficient permanence to warrant such a guide
as this.

The coverage and organization of this book correspond
closely to the course in Japanese bibliography offered at
Columbia University. Instruction at Columbia in the method-
ology of Far Eastern studies commenced more than thirty years
ago when L. Carrington Goodrich inaugurated a course in
Chinese bibliography. The companion course in Japanese
bibliography dates from 1938. I am deeply indebted to my
teachers in these courses, particularly Professor Goodrich,
Chi-chen Wang, C. Martin Wilbur, and Osamu Shimizu, for
their having imparted to me most of the principles and much
of the content here. To Dr. Shimizu I am doubly obligated,
for he gave generously of his time and advice in his present
position as head of the Japanese Section, Orientalia Division,
of the Library of Congress. Andrew Kuroda and Cho Sung
Yoon, also of the Library of Congress, performed further
valuable services in guiding my assistant and me through the
magnificent Japanese holdings of that institution. Library
staff members of the fine university collections which we
visited were invariably hospitable and helpful. These included
Charles Hamilton, Richard Irwin, and the staff of the East
Asiatic Library, the University of California at Berkeley; the
staff of the Japanese collection, the University of Michigan;
and the staff of the Chinese and Japanese Library, Harvard
University. Constance Winchell and her staff at the main

Reference Collection of the Columbia University Library answered numerous requests from us. We have been aided daily in countless ways by Howard Linton, Miwa Kai, Philip Yampolsky, Haruko Taketomo, and their fellow workers in the East Asian Library, Columbia University.

I should also like to acknowledge the aid and encouragement given to me by the following colleagues at my own and at other institutions: Hans Bielenstein, Enid Bishop, Albert Craig, Wm. Theodore de Bary, John W. Hall, Chih-tsing Hsia, Donald Keene, Eugene Langston, James Morley, Ivan I. Morris, Herbert Passin, Toshio Sawada, and Ichiro Shirato.

Marleigh Ryan did much of the research that resulted in the descriptions and other information in this book. In addition, she prepared initial drafts of Chapter 1, Chapter 6, and the appendices. The author takes full responsibility for the text in its final form, including any errors of fact or opinion that it may contain.

HERSCHEL WEBB

March, 1964

Contents

Contents xiii

Research in Japanese Sources: A Guide

1. Bibliography and General Reference

ASSUME that you, a student, librarian, or scholar, have been asked to prepare a written report on some recent event in Japanese history—say, the assassination of Socialist Party Chairman Asanuma Inejirō by a young rightist fanatic at a public political gathering on October 12, 1960. You might sensibly start with a survey of the coverage in the English-language press, for example by consulting the *New York Times Index* or the issues for surrounding dates of English-language papers published in Japan. It might also be fruitful to consult guides to current publications, particularly the *Readers' Guide to Periodical Literature*, to see if more comprehensive or interpretative accounts than those of the daily papers have been written in English. But having exhausted the materials in your own language, you would still probably have questions that can be answered only by referring to Japanese-language sources. Here again the most obvious place to look would be the daily newspapers, but with major events in Japan the coverage is apt to be so voluminous that efficient use of them requires a reference guide. Each of the three Japanese newspapers of national circulation publishes a yearbook, or *nenkan*, in the pages of which there appears a classified summary of the year's major news stories, a kind of functional index to that newspaper's coverage of each event. After the newspapers, you might turn to weekly and monthly periodicals, but here again you would need to approach the problem through a bibliographic guide—in this case, a guide to periodical literature. Are there published books which deal with the event? Yet another kind of bibliography, a list of current publications, will provide the answer.

So far each step in your research would have been cumbersome or totally impossible without basic bibliographic tools. With them it has been relatively easy, especially since in this case the subject is a recent event for which there exist a limited number of accounts all in easily predictable locations.

Had the subject been one from more remote history, the problem would have been harder, but it would still have been best to approach it by a number of well-defined and tested procedures. As an example of "low level" research into such a historical problem ("low level" in the sense that, while it puts together facts from a number of different places, it cannot be expected to uncover any completely new information), let us take the Battle of Sekigahara, on October 21, 1600, an event with which the rule of the Tokugawa dynasty of shoguns is often considered to have begun. As with the above example, it is best to begin with the material in Western languages. Newspapers will obviously be of no value, but other periodical literature, in the form of scholarly articles in learned journals, is likely to be very useful. For these, bibliographic guides exist. Some are classified by subject and others are merely lists of current publications. The same may be said of academic dissertations and other book-length studies in Western languages. For all these classes of materials the work of bibliographic compilation necessitates your knowing at the outset of your research the appropriate bibliographic materials.

All of these are discussed in this chapter, and in addition we treat certain other basic reference works without which you can scarcely begin the study of any topic about Japan. A newspaper account of Asanuma's death is not likely to explain to your satisfaction the political point of view that made him an object of controversy, but if you inspect the index to one of the newspaper yearbooks mentioned above, under the item "Shakai Minshu-tō"—Social Democratic Party—you will be led to interesting background information. The same procedure with an encyclopedia of modern history will yield some more. The same steps might be pursued for an understanding of the assassin's political connections or the nature of the political situation that brought Socialists and their enemies together in one public gathering.

Similarly, with the Battle of Sekigahara, the most elementary information is likely to be found in sources other than specific treatments. General encyclopedias, encyclopedias of history, and historical chronologies are works that you should turn to automatically whenever you start a new topic of research, large or small.

BIBLIOGRAPHIES OF WESTERN LANGUAGE MATERIALS. Until World War II there were so few works on Japan in Western languages that they could be listed in a single inclusive bibliography. This is a series begun in 1895 with a volume edited by Friedrich von Wenckstern listing all works published from the fifteenth century to 1893.[1] The series was continued by various compilers and includes materials published up to 1937.[2]

There is no single publication currently being issued which pretends to be as inclusive as the prewar "standard bibliography." The *Bibliography of Asian Studies* (*BAS*) is the most nearly complete of several series now being published, and it is fortunately the one most easily available for American students.

---

[1] *A Bibliography of the Japanese Empire* . . . *1859–93* (Leiden, 1895).

[2] For a complete listing of these titles see Hugh Borton *et al.*, eds., *A Selected List of Books and Articles on Japan* (rev. ed.; Cambridge, Mass., 1954), pp. 1–2.

A volume containing photostats of the cards prepared by Hans Praesent for *Bibliographie von Japan 1938–1943* is available at some libraries, including the Library of Congress. There are over 3,500 entries listing the German language publications issued in those years.

It is published annually as a regular issue of the *Journal of Asian Studies*. The series was begun in 1936.[3] A section on Bibliography and Reference in each issue of the *BAS* cites the other serial bibliographies of general coverage.

Careful study of these large lists is essential to ensure discovery of the lurking odd item of value that has so far eluded the attention of more specialized bibliographers. Trivia and ephemera abound in them, and they are cumbersome to use. They should be consulted without fail at some time in the pursuit of every research topic, but they are easiest to use when the student already has a firm grasp of his subject. For the preliminary stages of his study, he would do better to go to a selective bibliography prepared by a reputable specialist.

The best place to start is Borton's *A Selected List of Books and Articles on Japan*. It lists secondary studies and translations relating to a wide range of subjects, and often indicates with a brief comment those which are especially valuable. The opening section, on bibliographies, makes it the best guide to other lists of Western-language materials on Japan. The high quality and general availability of *A Selected List* make it unnecessary to repeat any of its contents here. Attention should be called, however, to some useful materials which have appeared since it was last issued in 1954.

1. A *List of Japanese Government Publications in European Languages 1945–1955* was issued in 1956 by the National Diet Library. It provides a convenient check list for students of recent events. It includes a catalog of SCAP publications.

2. A bibliography of Western-language works on Buddhism has been compiled by several reputable Japanese scholars.[4] It is

---

[3] The names of former editors and earlier titles of this bibliography can be found in Borton, pp. 2–3.

[4] Bandō Shōjun *et al.*, eds., *A Bibliography on Japanese Buddhism* (Tokyo, 1958).

selective rather than exhaustive. The items were carefully chosen, and the organization is systematic.

3. The office of the Meiji Shrine in Tokyo has issued a list of titles relating to Shinto studies,[5] useful despite the fact that many items are superficial. Originally compiled just before World War II, it has been brought up to date by an appendix of materials published between 1940 and 1952.

When the general and specialized bibliographies of Western-language materials have been exhausted, there still remain other fruitful sources of bibliographic information. One of the most obvious is a bibliography, annotated or otherwise, in some other scholar's book or article about a subject close to one's own.

Another source, useful primarily for material too recent to appear in the lists of specifically Japanese relevance, is the general guides to current publications. The laborious task of sifting publishers' lists has, since 1960, been made somewhat simpler by the introduction of the monthly *BPR: American Book Publishing Record*,[6] which gives titles and brief descriptions of all American books released in the preceding month.[7] *The International Index*[8] is the best source of information on scholarly articles, for it lists materials appearing in the leading journals of Asian studies as well as in other fields. The subject classification in this index facilitates its use. The coverage is more pertinent to scholars' interests than such general lists as the *Readers' Guide to Periodical Literature*. As a means of obtaining semidocumentary information on current events as well as a

[5] Katō Genchi *et al.*, eds., *A Bibliography of Shinto in Western Languages from Oldest Times Till 1952* (Tokyo, 1953).

[6] This is compiled by the R. R. Bowker Company, which also issues *Publishers' Weekly*, another useful guide.

[7] Other records of books currently in print are described in Constance M. Winchell, *Guide to Reference Books* (Chicago, 1951), pp. 21–23.

[8] *International Index: A Quarterly Guide to Periodical Literature in the Social Sciences and Humanities* (New Series: New York, from 1916).

source of publishing information, the *New York Times Index*[9] should not be overlooked.

The student of Japan should constantly keep himself informed of translations from Japanese into Western languages. *The Index Translationum*,[10] now issued annually by UNESCO, is a thorough record of such materials based on information furnished by the country in which the translation appears. In order to discover all the translations which have been done from Japanese, it is necessary to scan the lists for each contributing country. Despite this drawback, the series is very valuable, for it also provides an efficient source of information on what foreign works are being translated into Japanese, a matter of considerable interest to students of contemporary Japanese culture.[11]

For information on translations as well as on all other works of scholarship recently completed in America, the student is referred to two publications. The first is *Dissertation Abstracts*,[12] which contains summaries of essays submitted by doctoral candidates in certain American universities. Unfortunately there is no single subdivision for Oriental studies, and the reader must go to the various general categories to find information on his specialization. This deficiency is only partially compensated for by an author index. The annual *Index to*

---

[9] (New York, from 1913), now semimonthly, cumulated annually. Microfilms are available for indexes to the issues for the years 1851–58; 1860; and 1863–June 1905.

[10] *Index Translationum: International Bibliography of Translations* (Paris, International Institute of Intellectual Cooperation, 1932–40, 1948; UNESCO, from 1949).

[11] An exhaustive list of works translated into Japanese from 1868 to 1955 has been compiled by the National Diet Library under the title *Hon'yaku bungaku mokuroku* (Tokyo, 1959).

[12] *Dissertation Abstracts: Abstracts of Dissertations and Monographs in Microfilm* (Ann Arbor, from 1952), now monthly. This publication was formerly called *Microfilm Abstracts* (1938–51).

American Doctoral Dissertations[13] is a more inclusive work, listing all recipients of the degree for the previous year. Publications of more specific relevance to Japanese studies are *American Doctoral Dissertations on Asia, 1933-1962*[14] and *Columbia University Masters' Essays and Doctoral Dissertations on Asia, 1875-1956*.[15]

BIBLIOGRAPHIES OF JAPANESE BIBLIOGRAPHIES AND OTHER REFERENCE WORKS. To locate Japanese-language materials on a given subject it is necessary to refer to specialized or selective bibliographies. General exhaustive lists exist and have important uses of their own, but they are simply too voluminous to be of any help in compiling a working bibliography on a limited subject. Specialized lists, too, are numerous, but not so much so that they cannot be enumerated in the basic bibliographies of bibliographies and other reference works.

The best guide to reference books is *Nihon no sankō tosho*.[16] It describes systematically bibliographies, linguistic and biographical dictionaries, yearbooks, historical chronologies, and other types of basic works. It seems to render obsolete the earlier annotated bibliographies of reference books, [*Kenkyū chōsa*] *Sankō bunken sōran*[17] and *Sankō tosho no kaidai*.[18] Lacking any of these, the student may consult with profit the *Sankō tosho sōgō mokuroku* issued in 1955 by the National Diet Library. As its name implies, this is merely a systematic list of the

---

[13] (Ann Arbor, from 1957). The Index was formerly issued under the title *Doctoral Dissertations Accepted by American Universities* (New York, 1934–55).

[14] Curtis W. Stucki, ed. (Ithaca, 1963).

[15] Compiled by the East Asiatic Library, Columbia University (New York, 1957). The student is also referred to the Japan section of the publication entitled *External Research: A List of Studies Currently in Progress* compiled by the Office of Intelligence Research and Analysis, U.S. Department of State. The same office is responsible for *External Research: A List of Recently Completed Studies*, which has a section on East Asia. Both of these government publications are currently being issued.

[16] Nihon no Sankō Tosho Henshū Iin-kai, comp. (Tokyo, 1962).

[17] Hatano Ken'ichi and Yayoshi Mitsunaga, eds. (Tokyo, 1934).

[18] Yayoshi Mitsunaga, ed. (Tokyo, 1955).

library's holdings in reference books and does not contain any critical discussion of their value. It has the additional disadvantage of being very difficult to read, since it is a photographic reproduction of a handwritten list.

A small but highly critical guide to reference works has been compiled by the Kokusai Bunka Shinkokai[19] as the first in a projected series of ten bibliographies on various fields. The notes contain historical and technical descriptions which are both interesting and informative, and very recent publications are included. UNESCO has sponsored a *Directory of Reference Works Published in Asia*,[20] which lists, without additional criticism or evaluation, many Japanese-language books, including some neglected by other sources.

The standard bibliography of published bibliographies is Amano Keitarō's [*Hompō*] *Shoshi no shoshi*. Although this book, compiled in 1933, is now out of date, there is no other single source which contains as much information on both premodern and modern works of that kind. One must consult either guides to general reference books like those mentioned above or studies of limited fields to discover the titles of pertinent bibliographies published since that date.

SOME SPECIALIZED BIBLIOGRAPHIES. Among current bibliographies one of the most rewarding is the series now being issued annually under the title *Keizai-shi bunken*.[21] It is compiled under the supervision of Honjō Eijirō, one of Japan's leading economic historians. The material included is of far

---

[19] *K. B. S. Bibliography of Standard Reference Books for Japanese Studies,* Vol. 1: *Generalia* (Tokyo, 1959).

[20] P. K. Garde, ed. (Paris, 1956).

[21] (Tokyo, from 1955). A continuous bibliographical survey of the field can be made by using this and the works listed below, all edited by Honjō:

> [*Kaihan*] *Nihon keizai-shi bunken* (Tokyo, 1933)
> *Nihon keizai-shi shin bunken* (Tokyo, 1942)
> *Nihon keizai-shi dai-san bunken* (Tokyo, 1953)
> *Keizai-shi nenkan* (3 vols.; Tokyo, 1955–56).

broader application than the name of the series would imply; it is, in fact, an annotated list of historical writings, including reference books, collections of primary materials, and secondary sources.

Since 1950, the Center for Japanese Studies at the University of Michigan has been issuing a group of annotated bibliographies of primary and secondary materials. The entries in each volume are carefully selected and described on the basis of their significance to scholarly research. The numbers issued to date relate to Japanese political science, dialects, history, economics, geography, religion and philosophy, literature, language, sociology, and Far Eastern archaeology and ethnology. Virtually all of the works listed are in the Japanese language.

Although each of the bibliographies attempts to present a thorough review of basic reference materials, two are of special importance in this respect. John W. Hall's *Japanese History*[22] is an indispensable guide to secondary work dealing with the premodern period. "History" is interpreted in its broadest sense to include intellectual and cultural developments as well as economic and political systems. The accurate and concise descriptions are extremely helpful, evaluating the material in terms of its usefulness to a historian.

Another item in the Michigan series is Robert E. Ward's bibliography of books, articles, documents, and reference works relevant to the study of political science since 1868.[23] Its subsections contain entries on the constitution, political parties, elections, the legal system, and the various branches of the government, as well as on general political theory and political history. Professor Hall's bibliography has been

---

[22] *Japanese History: A Guide to Japanese Reference and Research Materials* (Ann Arbor, 1954).

[23] Robert E. Ward and Hajime Watanabe, eds., *Japanese Political Science: A Guide to Japanese Reference and Research Materials* (rev. ed.; Ann Arbor, 1962).

indexed by the School of Oriental Studies of Canberra University College in Australia, as has the earlier (1950) edition of Professor Ward's. These indexes are not for sale but copies of them have been deposited in certain American university libraries.

A valuable bibliography of Japanese language materials relating to a more specialized field of political science is Cecil H. Uyehara's *Leftwing Social Movements in Japan*, published in Tokyo in 1959. The author has attempted to present items applicable to the study of the whole range of leftist opinion from the most moderate to the most radical. With the exception of a few earlier titles, the materials date from the period between World War I and 1956. Many pre-World War II government documents which were formerly classified and which were the result of reports and studies made by the secret police are described here for the first time. Wherever possible, the location of each item is given, thereby facilitating the use of this extensive list as a key to the vast store of primary and secondary material available in the United States on this aspect of modern Japanese history.

EXHAUSTIVE LISTS OF CURRENT PUBLICATIONS. It is, of course, very difficult to select Japanese-language materials wisely from exhaustive lists, but there are instances in which it is necessary to be aware of every title relevant to a given topic. To obtain this knowledge, one may use a class of books called *shuppan nenkan*, or publishers' yearbooks, which give the titles and some limited additional information about works published in the preceding year. Such yearbooks have been issued since about 1926 under a variety of titles by various publishers. They are primarily useful to book dealers and librarians who must keep abreast of information from the publishing world. The student, too, can obtain a good survey being done in his field by referring to the section of the yearbook relating to it. In addition, if he has reason to believe that a book of interest to him has been published and he is not sure of its exact title or its author's name, careful scrutiny of a yearbook may uncover it for him.[24]

In recent years, the government has been endeavoring to compile an exhaustive record of all books, magazines, films, slides, etc., published in Japan and deposited in the National Diet Library. The series is called *Zen-Nihon shuppan-butsu sō-mokuroku*.[25] Its coverage is more extensive than that of the *shuppan nenkan*. It includes published materials not offered for sale to the public, like government documents and reports, and compilations by private societies and research institutions. Unfortunately, it is always several years behind and therefore does not obviate the use of the privately published yearbook.

A thorough survey of government publications can be made by consulting the *Kanchō kankō-butsu sōgō mokuroku*.[26] Except for the period from September of 1943 to September, 1945, the series lists all official publications since 1927. There has been an enormous increase in the output of all manner of specialized reports and statistical surveys by the various organs of the government. Some are deposited in the National Diet Library, and there are additional copies in the libraries of the issuing authorities. This catalog indicates the name of the branch responsible for the book or article and analyzes the contents of those continuing publications which contain valuable research materials.

---

[24] The current series is entitled simply *Shuppan nenkan* and has been published in Tokyo by the Shuppan Nyūsu-sha since 1951. See Hatano and Yayoshi for earlier series.

[25] The series covers works published since 1948, and has been published in Tokyo ever since 1951.

[26] Published by the Kokuritsu Kokkai Tosho-kan (Tokyo, from 1952). Earlier versions bore the titles:

> *Kanchō kankō tosho mokuroku* (Tokyo, 1927–38), quarterly
> *Kanchō kankō tosho geppō* (Tokyo, 1938–43).

PUBLISHED LIBRARY CATALOGS. The question naturally arises as to how to find out about a work published prior to the years covered by these various general book lists. Often the only source of such information is one of the catalogs published by many leading Japanese libraries.[27] Upon completion, the *Shiryō Hensan-jo tosho mokuroku*[28] will be one of the most valuable works of this kind. Descriptions of the manuscripts and printed primary and secondary sources used in the compilation of the monumental studies edited by this group will be available in a convenient form for the first time.

A classified catalog of the acquisitions of the National Diet Library from 1945 to 1958[29] is currently being published. It serves as a continuation of the catalogs issued by the library's predecessors. It will be supplemented in the future by an annual acquisitions list and a cumulated edition every five years.

INDEXES TO PERIODICAL LITERATURE. The student should regularly scan current Japanese periodicals to keep himself informed of the latest scholarship in his field. The Ministry of Education has compiled a list of learned journals[30] which will give him the titles of those pertinent to his studies.

The National Diet Library compiles a quarterly index of magazines and government periodicals.[31] There are currently

---

[27] For an annotated bibliography of library catalogs see Joseph K. Yamagiwa, ed., *Japanese Language Studies in the Shōwa Period: A Guide to Japanese Reference and Research Materials* (Ann Arbor, 1961), pp. 1–5.

Two sources are needed to discover the names and locations of all the libraries in Japan:

Nihon Gakugei Kaigi, ed., *Nihon tosho-kan sōran* (Tokyo, 1954)
Semmon tosho-kan kyōgi-kai, ed., *Chōsa kikan tosho-kan sōran* (Tokyo, 1956).

[28] [*Tōkyō Daigaku*] *Shiryō Hensan-jo tosho mokuroku* (Tokyo, from 1960).

[29] [*Kokuritsu Kokkai Tosho-kan*] *Zōsho mokuroku* (Tokyo, from 1960).

[30] *Bibliographical List of Japanese Learned Journals: Humanities & Social Sciences* (Tokyo, 1959).

[31] *Zasshi kiji sakuin: Jimbun kagaku-hen* (Tokyo, from 1949); *Shizen kagaku-hen* (from 1950).

two series being printed, one for the humanities and social sciences and another for the natural sciences. The issue of the former series for January-March, 1960, indexes some 399 publications, including many mentioned but not analyzed in the *Kanchō kankō-butsu sōgō mokuroku*. Each issue can be used to determine what material is available on a certain topic and what a certain author has written.

BASIC REFERENCE WORKS. Without doubt a general encyclopedia is the most useful of all basic reference tools. It performs most of the same functions as a biographical dictionary, a gazetteer, or a whole library of special encyclopedias and treatises on particular subjects, though of course not in the same detail. The Heibon-sha company has published the two most up to date of the large works of this class.[32]

Very concise information of the same kind is offered in the same company's *Dai jiten*.[33] In the main this is a linguistic dictionary, but an extraordinarily large and complete one. Inasmuch as all of the entries are in a single alphabetical arrangement, the student may locate words readily in it even if he finds himself in the embarrassing but common predicament of not knowing whether what he is looking for is a man's name, a book title, or the name of a popular kimono shop of the nineteenth century.

The *nenkan*, or yearbooks, published by Japanese newspapers and wire services have been mentioned at the beginning of this chapter. They are in effect encyclopedias of current events. Their coverage is broad, including among others, politics, vital statistics, business news, social and intellectual currents, and sports. Items are not alphabetical, but indexes are usually complete and reliable. Particular attention should be drawn to

---

[32] *Dai hyakka jiten* (28 vols.; Tokyo, 1931–35, Supplements 1939, 1950) (A reduced-type edition was published in 1950.) and *Sekai dai hyakka jiten* (32 vols.; Tokyo, 1959).

[33] (26 vols.; Tokyo, 1934–36). There is a reduced-type edition in 13 volumes.

the summaries of important news events of the year, the necrologies, and the generous statistical tables that these publications contain.[34]

---

[34] *Asahi nenkan* (Osaka, from 1923) is the most frequently referred to, owing to the prestige of the newspaper.

2. Problems Concerning Dates, Time, and Chronology

SINCE January 1, 1873, the Japanese have used the Gregorian calendar. The·only respect in which their method for designating dates differs from ours is that instead of reckoning years in relation to the Christian era, they number them serially from the one in which a reigning emperor ascended the throne. Hence, October 12, 1960, was identical with the Japanese date 昭和三十五年十月十二日—the twelfth day of the tenth month of the thirty-fifth year of Shōwa.

However, in dealing with Japanese measurements of time before 1873 one encounters numerous problems. Some of these arise from the fact that the nomenclature used was complex, there often being several different ways of referring to a single unit of the civil calendar. More fundamental difficulties result from the fact that the official Japanese calendar was a *lunar calendar*. That is to say, it was based on completely different principles from those of the solar calendars which the Western world has used for civil purposes since Roman times.

SOLAR AND LUNAR CALENDARS. The differences between solar and lunar calendars can best be understood by reference to the most important feature which they share: both systems take as their basic counting units the *year*, corresponding with greater or less exactitude to the period of the earth's revolution around the sun, and the *month*, approximating the period of the moon's revolution around the earth. Astronomers describe the motions of these heavenly bodies with mathematical accuracy and thereby define units of time which one may call the *natural year* and the *natural month*, or *lunation*. Neither of these units is satisfactory for social purposes, for neither contains a whole number of days, and one natural year does not contain a whole number of natural months.

Civil calendars remedy these defects in a variety of ways. A solar calendar is one which takes as its main basis for measuring time the natural year, modifying it for civil purposes only to the extent of reckoning calendar years as whole numbers of days (either 365 or 366). If the leap years in such a calendar are carefully apportioned, it will never deviate far from the year of nature. The vernal equinox will fall on or about March 21 in our own solar calendar until the end of time, unless the astronomers have miscalculated.

Inasmuch as the number of natural months in a natural year is an unwieldy fraction somewhere between twelve and thirteen, societies with solar calendars customarily ignore the lunation as a practical unit for measuring time. The "month" used for civil purposes in these calendars is merely one of twelve more or less equal divisions of a civil year.

Lunar calendars are devised to answer the same problems, but they do so in a completely different way. Their basic unit of measurement is a civil month, which differs from the lunation only to the degree necessary to ensure that each contains a whole number of days (twenty-nine or thirty). A lunar calendar, properly constructed, is a close reflection of the phases of the moon. A full moon occurs on or about the same day of every civil month. In the Chinese and Japanese civil calendar, a new moon occurred on the first day of the month.

In order that each civil year should contain a whole number of months, it deviated considerably from the natural year. Twelve months totaled about 354 days—nearly two weeks short of a natural year—while thirteen months—about 383 days—was even wider of the mark. The Chinese and Japanese civil year normally contained twelve months, but in order to assure that there would be a rough correspondence between a certain month of the civil year and a certain season of the natural year, a thirteenth month was added, or *intercalated*, in some years. This combination of features—close correspondence between civil and natural months plus inexact correspondence between civil and natural years—marks the essential difference between the old Japanese lunar calendar and the solar calendar of the Western world.

THE OLD SOLAR CALENDAR. The Japanese civil calendar had the virtues of any arbitrary system for the reckoning of dates, but aside from that the most that can be said for it was that it offered an excellent guide to the best evenings for moon viewing. For agricultural purposes it was useless. Farmers needed a calendar that would tell them the best times for planting and harvest, activities that followed the seasons of the natural year. In short, they needed a solar calendar. Ancient Chinese astronomers provided one which was both simple and accurate, and it has been in use among farmers ever since, although it has never been used to reckon dates officially. The nomenclature of the old solar calendar is still in common use among Japanese, and its workings must be understood for the bearing which they had on the operation of the official lunar calendar.

The natural year was measured by reference to the period between two successive occurrences of the winter solstice (*tōji* 冬至 in Japanese). In fact the winter solstice was not taken as the *beginning* of the solar year; it was the midpoint of the first of twelve divisions of the year. Each of these divisions was of absolutely equal duration. Each, that is, contained a fractional number of days—about 30.44. The Japanese word for one of these divisions of the old solar calendar is *setsu* 節. The beginning of a *setsu* is known as *nyū-setsu* 入節, and the midpoint of a *setsu* is known as *chūsetsu* 中節. As the winter solstice marked the first *chūsetsu* of the solar year, the first *nyūsetsu*, which began the year, occurred about fifteen days earlier, approximately December 6 in the Gregorian calendar.

Each *nyūsetsu* and *chūsetsu* had its own name, often highly expressive of weather or agricultural phenomena. These twenty-four points in the old solar calendar correspond very closely to dates of the Gregorian calendar; any deviation is a result of the fact that a point in the Gregorian system itself sometimes differs by as much as a whole day from the corresponding point in the natural solar year.

THE OLD CIVIL CALENDAR. As has been mentioned above, the civil calendar of Japan was lunar and corresponded only inexactly to the seasons of the natural year. Nevertheless, in order that there be at least a rough correspondence, calendar makers made use of certain devices relating to the old solar calendar just described. Civil months in the Japanese calendar were numbered from one to twelve, and the numbers were derived according to the following formula. The lunar month containing the first *chūsetsu* (which was of course the winter solstice, a point in the solar year) was always numbered the eleventh of the civil year. (It was not, unfortunately, the first civil month, for intriguing but irrelevant reasons.) Similarly, the civil month including the second *chūsetsu* was the twelfth, and that containing the third *chūsetsu*, which fell about February 19 in the Gregorian calendar, was the first month—*shōgatsu* 正月. Hence the rule for determining the beginning of the Japanese civil year: it fell on the first new moon preceding the third *chūsetsu* of the solar year. The exact Gregorian date for the Japanese New Year varied, but it was always between January 21 and February 19.

Intercalation of additional months was determined in the

following way. Some civil months contained no *chūsetsu*, for the period between successive *chūsetsu* was about one day longer than the lunation that determined a civil month. If a *chūsetsu* fell within a few hours immediately preceding a new moon, the next *chūsetsu* fell just *after* the next new moon. In such a case, the whole intervening civil month was called intercalary —*jun* 閏—and took its number from the preceding civil month. Thus, a month designated as intercalary third—*jun-sangatsu* 閏三月—fell between the third and the fourth month of the civil calendar. An intercalation occurred regularly about one month out of every thirty.

This brief description cannot take into account the minor irregularities in the Japanese civil calendar. The Japanese did not invent the system, but adopted it, ready-made, from China in 604. The astronomical and mathematical work on which it depended had been done long since, and Chinese and Japanese of later times normally applied formulas, rather than relying on direct astronomical observations, for intercalation and for determining when to start a new month. If the formulas were slightly inaccurate, a month might be intercalated too soon or too late, or the first day of a civil month might fall a day before or after the appearance of a new moon. Such variations from the ideal system described in the above paragraphs were thought to necessitate correction of the calendar. Invariably the Chinese devised corrections first, the Japanese not following suit for some years or centuries afterward. As a consequence, the Chinese and Japanese civil calendars occasionally differed in the designation for a day or a month, and one must be careful not to assume exact correspondence between them.

It also follows that the conversion of a Japanese lunar date to its Gregorian equivalent is a problem for historians rather than astronomers. Excellent records have been kept of the exact duration of every civil month and year, and these supply

the information in the calendrical conversion tables which
modern scholars have compiled. There are three of these for
Japanese dates. The earliest, that of Bramsen,[1] contains
inaccuracies and has probably been superseded by the other
two: *Sansei sōran*,[2] an official publication, and *Japanese
Chronological Tables* by Paul Tsuchihashi, issued in 1952. Both
of these give the Western date corresponding to the first day
of every Japanese civil month. The instructions below for the
conversion of dates may be used for any of these three
tables.[3]

THE PARTS OF A DATE. A date in the Japanese lunar
calendar conveys three pieces of information: the year, the
month, and the day of the month. Let us examine each of
these three elements in turn, at the same time considering the
most expeditious methods of ascertaining the equivalents in the
Western calendar.

YEAR DESIGNATIONS. There are four different methods for
specifying a year of the Japanese civil calendar. (1) One
consists of the name of a calendrical era—or *nengō* 年号—and
the number of a year within the era. Take for example the
year 慶長五年—fifth year of Keichō—in which the Battle of
Sekigahara occurred. Keichō was an era which began in 1596.
(2) The fifth year of Keichō might also be called 庚子年
(pronounced either *Kōshi no toshi* or *Kanoe-ne no toshi*). This
particular designation always specifies the thirty-seventh year
of a cycle, in this case the cycle that began in 1564. (3) The
same year might also be designated as the year 2260 of a
continuing era dated from 660 B.C., the legendary date of the

---

[1] William Bramsen, *Japanese Chronological Tables* (Tokyo, 1880).

[2] Naimushō Chiri-kyoku (Tokyo, 1932).

[3] A table of correspondences for *each day* of the Chinese and Japanese lunar
calendars and its Gregorian equivalent has been published for the years 1700–1911.
It is Gaimushō Bunsho-ka, comp., *Nihon gaikō bunsho: Kindai in-yō-reki taishō-hyō*
(Tokyo; preface, 1951).

founding of the Japanese imperial dynasty. The word *kigen*
紀元—the beginning of the dynasty—is sometimes prefixed
to such dates to differentiate them from years of the Christian
era. (4) A fourth method, used only for dates in early Japanese
history, identifies a year by its number in the reign of an
emperor. All four methods require some explanation, if the
student is to interpret them readily and accurately.

NENGŌ. The normal method for identifying dates in the
Japanese calendar involves the use of relatively brief calendrical
eras known as *nengō*. This feature of the calendar was an
imitation of Chinese practice, but the Japanese did not adopt
it until 645, some decades after the first use of the Chinese
calendar in Japan. The first Japanese era name, commemor-
ating the revolutionary political changes of that year, was
Taika—or Great Reform. The practice fell out of official use
in the latter part of the seventh century, but was adopted
again in 701 and has been in continuous use ever since.

The Japanese imperial court made the decisions when to
declare a new era and what to call it. Customarily, though
not invariably, a new era was declared within a year or two
after the accession of a new emperor. At two points in each
sexagenary cycle, the first year and the fifty-eighth, which were
thought to be auspicious, a new era was usually proclaimed.
In addition, the era might be changed for a variety of other
reasons—for example, after some felicitous or unlucky
event.

One should not refer to premodern *nengō* as "reign names."
Only after 1868 did the Japanese adopt the practice of including the entire reign of an emperor in one era. Meiji, the
era proclaimed in that year, continued until the death of the
reigning sovereign in 1912. His son's reign, coterminous with
the Taishō era, lasted until December 25, 1926, when the
present reign, the Shōwa calendrical era, began. Meiji and
later *nengō* differ from all previous ones in that they have been

or will be designated as official posthumous names of the emperors whose reigns they commemorate.

The name of an era might indicate the reason for its adoption, as in the case of the Wadō 和銅 era (701-704), proclaimed because the discovery of copper deposits in Japan allowed work to be begun on the great image of the Buddha in Nara. More often, however, the literal significance of a *nengō* is neither obvious from its appearance nor realized generally by Japanese people. For the most part, the characters are of pleasant connotation and allude to classical tags from the ethical literature of Chinese Confucianism. Scholars writing in English rarely translate them into English words, but merely transcribe them into the Roman alphabet.

The proclamation of a new era—*kaigen* 改元—could occur at any time in the civil year. It is customary among scholars, however, to refer to the entire year in which a new era began, including dates before the change, as the first year—*gannen* 元年 —of the new era, though of course one encounters instances in contemporary documents of dating by the preceding *nengō*. One even finds year designations which never officially existed at all. For example, 1927 was officially the second year of Shōwa, but most periodicals dated January of that year bear the designation Taishō sixteen. The explanation is obvious: the Shōwa *nengō* was not proclaimed until Christmas Day, 1926, after most publishers of magazines had sent their January issues to press.

It is easy to find the Western equivalent of a year numbered within a *nengō* if one knows when the era was proclaimed. Many sources give initial and terminal years for Japanese *nengō*. Bramsen's and Tsuchihashi's conversion tables are two obvious places to look, and historical encyclopedias give authoritative information as to the exact dates when the *nengō* were changed. If you are puzzled about the pronunciation of a *nengō*, remember that the characters of a *nengō* are invariably pronounced according to one or another of their Sino-Japanese—*on*—readings.[4]

To find the Western year in which a Japanese year began, take the Western year in which the *first* year of the *nengō* began, subtract one (to obtain the number of a hypothetical "zero" year) and add the number of the Japanese year within the *nengō*.

UNOFFICIAL NENGŌ. Occasionally in premodern works one comes upon era designations that were never officially adopted by the Japanese court. These are known as *shi-nengō* 私年号—private, or unofficial, *nengō*. The exact ways in which they came into being are various and often difficult to determine. There are numerous tables which indicate the initial years (if they are known) for *shi-nengō*. See, for example, those in *Nihon-shi jiten*.[5] Students of Japanese art history often see references to the *shi-nengō* Hakuhō 白鳳, denoting the period from 673 to 686, when no official *nengō* was in use.

During the schism of the imperial dynasty from 1338 to 1393 both the Northern (Kyoto) Court and the rival Southern (Yoshino) Court reckoned dates according to their own *nengō*. The Southern Court is now regarded as the legitimate one, so its *nengō* are usually used today to date events within that period, but one still finds dates according to the Northern Court's *nengō*. Inclusive dates for these *nengō* will be found in most of the sources for those now regarded as official.

THE SEXAGENARY CYCLE. In addition to cardinal numerals, the Chinese and Japanese employ two sets of terms for purposes of enumeration. One of these sets contains ten terms and is known as *jikkan* 十干—the ten stems. The other

---

[4] Perhaps the most authoritative source on the pronunciation of *nengō* as well as other pertinent information about them is Morimoto Kakuzō's *Nihon nengō taikan* (Tokyo, 1933).

[5] Kyōto Daigaku Bungaku-bu Kokushi Kenkyū-shitsu, comp. [*Kaitei zōho*] *Nihon-shi jiten* (Tokyo, 1960).

contains twelve terms and is called *jūnishi* 十二支—the twelve branches. The characters, pronunciations, and original meanings of these terms need not concern us here. They are discussed in numerous places, most conveniently, perhaps, the introduction to Rose-Innes's *Beginner's Dictionary of Chinese-Japanese Characters*.

Since remote antiquity, the Far Eastern peoples have used these two sets of terms to enumerate years (and other units) of their civil calendar. When both series are used together they form a greater cycle of sixty terms, as sixty is the least common multiple of ten and twelve. The first term in the sexagenary cycle is formed of the first stem and the first branch, followed by the second stem and second branch, and so on. The eleventh term consists of the first stem and the eleventh branch, the twelfth term the second stem and twelfth branch, and the thirteenth term the third stem and first branch.

Individual sixty-year cycles have no names, but dates which are designated by cyclical signs generally include the appropriate *nengō* as well. In rare cases, as for example paintings and works of sculpture, one may find no indication of a date except the cyclical designation of a year. In these cases stylistic or archaeological evidence must be used to determine the particular cycle to which the designation applies.

Students who do much work with premodern Japanese historical sources would do well to memorize the stems and branches in their proper order, and to keep in mind some one memorable year which began a cycle, for purposes of ready calculation to any other. (The year 604, in which the Japanese officially adopted the Chinese calendar, was the first of a cycle. The year 1924 began the present one; and the Orwellian 1984 will begin another.) Each of the ten stems corresponds to a certain final digit in the number of a year in the Christian era. *Kō* 甲, the first stem, always appears in the sexagenary designation for a year of the Western calendar ending in the digit 4 (1944, 1954, 1964, etc.). Memorization of a few basic principles of this kind will save one many trips to a conversion table. For example, one may find a reference to the year 元禄甲戌年 and know of the Genroku era only that it included the year 1700. The first stem 甲 will indicate that the year might have been 1694 or 1704, while the eleventh branch 戌 will pinpoint it exactly. The year 1684 began a cycle; therefore 1694 was the eleventh year within it, and the only year near the turn of the eighteenth century that could correspond to the cyclical designation 甲戌. Of course there are other ways of finding the same information. *Sansei sōran* gives the cyclical designation for every year of the Japanese calendar.

THE JAPANESE CONTINUING ERA. This method of designating years is easiest to interpret, but also least frequently used. To find the Western equivalent for a year, simply subtract 660 from the number. (For dates B.C. subtract the number of the Japanese year from 661.) Remember that the Western year will not correspond exactly to the Japanese year, if the latter is before 2533 (A.D. 1873), but will be the one that started between nineteen and forty-nine days before the beginning of the Japanese civil year.

DESIGNATION BY YEAR OF REIGN. For dates of the seventh century and earlier, when official *nengō* did not exist, years may be designated by number within the reign of an emperor. In this case the official posthumous name of the emperor is used, and it is usually followed by the word *Tennō* 天皇, to distinguish the designation from a true *nengō*. For example, the seventh year of the reign of Suiko, which is written in Japanese 推古天皇七年, is equivalent to 600/601. This system appears similar to that for assigning *nengō* today. However, it differs in one important respect. The "first year" of a reign is taken, for calendrical purposes, to be the first full calendar year *after* the emperor's accession, the ceremony known in Japanese as *senso* 践祚, rather than the year in which the accession took place, as with *nengō* today. Take, for example, the case of the Emperor Tenchi. While he actually began to rule in 662, his ceremony of accession did not occur until 667. The "first year," for calendrical purposes, of his reign is therefore 668/669. To calculate the Western equivalent of a Japanese year identified in this way, one must first find the year of the emperor's accession, then add the number of the Japanese year. *Sansei sōran* is an authoritative source for the same information.

MONTH DESIGNATIONS. All civil months (except the first, which is usually known as *shōgatsu* 正月) are designated by number, or if intercalary, by the character *jun* 閏 plus the name of the preceding month. Terms of the sexagenary cycle could theoretically be applied to months, but almost never were, in practice.

In addition to their formal Sino-Japanese names (*shōgatsu, nigatsu, sangatsu,* etc.), the months had informal or poetic ones of native Japanese origin, as follows:

1.	*Mutsuki*	7.	*Fuzuki*
2.	*Kisaragi*	8.	*Hazuki*
3.	*Yayoi*	9.	*Nagazuki*
4.	*Uzuki*	10.	*Kannazuki*
5.	*Satsuki*	11.	*Shimotsuki*
6.	*Minatsuki*	12.	*Shiwasu*

These names are rarely used as parts of full dates.

Calendrical tables give the Western date corresponding to the first day of the Japanese month. They also indicate the duration of the month, which was either twenty-nine or thirty days. Tsuchihashi's tables convey the latter information by distinctions of typography, while *Sansei sōran*, in common with premodern calendars, does so by the use of the code characters *dai* 大—big—and *shō* 小—little.

Formal histories of premodern Japan sometimes included as

part of a date the word for the season of the year. This information has little practical value for dating purposes. Spring was considered to contain the first three civil months, summer the next three, and so on. An intercalary month was always considered to belong to the same season as the month preceding it.

DAY DESIGNATIONS. Days of a civil month are numbered in Japanese, so they will give no trouble in converting to Western equivalents. The character 朔 sometimes appears, especially in older sources, instead of 一日, for *tsuitachi*—the first day of a month—and the designation 晦 for *misoka*, which was the last day of a month, whether the twenty-ninth or the thirtieth. One recommended method of ensuring accuracy in converting to a Western date is as follows. Write the Japanese date (a) in the manner indicated below, on the left-hand side of a sheet of paper. Immediately under it write the date of the first day of the same Japanese month (b). Find in a conversion table the Western date corresponding to the first day of the Japanese month and copy it on the right-hand side of the page immediately opposite its Japanese equivalent (c). Subtract (b) from (a) to find the number of days (d) which you will have to add to (c) to give the answer you require (e). If your answer is a date which did not exist in the Western calendar (as in Example 2 below), subtract the number of days in the month labeled in your date (e) from the number indicated in that line as the day of the month, and label your corrected answer (f) with the name of the following month of the Western calendar.

If a day is identified by its position in the sexagenary cycle, you must find in a conversion table the cyclical designation of the first day of the Japanese civil month and proceed from there. The Tsuchihashi tables provide a formula for determining the numbered date in the Japanese month, and *Sansei sōran* supplies the same information by means of a

mechanical device (enclosed inside the back cover) consisting
of three concentric wheels. Whatever method you use, you
should find the Japanese numbered date before you start the
conversion into the Western calendar.

	YEAR	MONTH	DAY	YEAR	MONTH	DAY
Example 1						
(a) *Keichō*	5	9	15			
(b) *Keichō*	5	9	1	(c) 1600	October	7
(d)			14 days		plus	14
						—
				(e) 1600	October	21
Example 2						
(a) *Genroku*	6	12	29			
(b) *Genroku*	6	12	1	(c) 1693	December	27
			—			
(d)			28 days		plus	28
						—
				(e) 1693	December	55
					minus	31
						—
				(f) 1694	January	24

JULIAN AND GREGORIAN DATES. The civil calendar used
in all Christian countries up to the sixteenth century is known
as the Julian calendar, or Old Style (O.S.). A Papal decree
of 1582 established for Roman Catholic countries the New
Style (N.S.), or Gregorian calendar, which was a slightly
more accurate reflection of the natural solar year. English-
speaking countries did not adopt the Gregorian system until
1752, and the Julian calendar was still in use in Russia and
other areas of eastern Europe until after World War I.

The Japanese calendrical tables cited above differ as to
which of the two Western calendars they use in converting
Japanese dates of a given period. Students should be very

careful to notice the exact rules adopted in the tables which they consult. It is necessary to make reasonable and consistent rules in deciding which Western calendar to use. The following principles may help:

For dates through October 15, 1582—N.S. (October 4—O.S.): Normally convert to the Julian calendar. Only in very special cases is a Gregorian date justified. For example, data on solar or seasonal phenomena might be more meaningful if expressed in Gregorian terms, which correspond more closely to the natural year than do those of the Old Style.

For dates between 1582 and 1752: *The Harvard Guide to American History* (page 93) offers a convenient rule which may be applied in some cases to the conversion of Japanese dates. Use whichever calendar was current in the country or society with which you are dealing. For example, if you find references with Japanese dates to the Japanese mission to Rome of 1615, convert them to dates that would have been used in Rome, that is, Gregorian. If you make use of both Japanese and English sources dealing with the English-Japanese trade in the seventeenth century, it is most convenient to convert Japanese dates to the Julian calendar, which was in use among the English of that time. Where no guides of that kind are available, and in most cases they will not be, you must make your own rule; but be consistent and *describe your practice*.

For dates after 1752: The only justification for using Julian dates would be to accord with those which one might find in Russian sources.

TIMES OF DAY. Japan lies in a standard time zone which mariners call "plus nine." That is, standard time in that zone is always nine hours later than it is at the Greenwich meridian, and hence fourteen hours later than in New York, which is in zone "minus five." The difference in hour usually makes for a difference in date. For example, the Pearl Harbor attack that began the Pacific war occurred on December 7, 1941, Hawaii time, but December 8 Japanese time. In dating such events, scholars tend to use the local time of the place where the action of their narrative centers, and to describe their practice if it would otherwise be ambiguous.

Until the Meiji period, when the Western system for telling time came into general use, the Japanese described times of day in two different ways, neither of them applied with any great precision. One of these made use of the twelve branches, which have been referred to above in the paragraphs describing the sexagenary signs. Starting from a point halfway between sunset and sunrise, the period until dawn was divided into three equal parts of about two hours each, which were labeled with the first three of the twelve branches. *Ne* 子—the hour of the rat—corresponded to the period from roughly 12:00 midnight to 2:00 A.M., and so on. The next six signs represented equal divisions of the period from sunrise to sunset. The final three signs refer to equal parts of the first half of the period from sunset to sunrise. Sometimes a cyclical sign might be used for the *beginning* of a period, rather than its whole duration. Hence, in modern Japanese the words for A.M. and P.M. are *gozen* 午前 and *gogo* 午後, which mean literally before and after the hour of the horse. The character 午 (*go* or *uma*) is the seventh of the twelve branches.

The other system divided the day into the same twelve parts, but assigned numbers to them. The "hour of the rat" might also be called the ninth hour (*kokunotsu-doki* 九ツ時). The next period was the eighth hour, the next the seventh, and so on, counting backward until the last period of the forenoon, which was the fourth hour. For times of day from (roughly) noon to midnight, the same six numbers were used over again, beginning with nine and running back to four. No one is willing to commit himself as to just how this mystifying system got started. One plausible theory has it that the "hours" were at one time counted by multiples of nine (9, 18, 27, 36, 45, and 54), representing the number of drum strokes used to indicate them, and that later generations contracted the appellations for them by dropping the "tens" digit.[6]

[6] Yamaguchi Ryūji, *Nihon no tokei* (2nd rev. ed.; Tokyo, 1950).

3. Weights, Measures, Monetary Units, and Statistics

In this chapter we deal with various systems of measurement, including the measurement of economic value, as well as the related matter of ascertaining economic, demographic, and other kinds of statistics. Many problems in these matters are very easy and in fact require no knowledge of Japanese at all; others are so difficult that they lie completely beyond the scope of this book. Our practice in dealing with cases of the latter kind will be simply to explain some of the reasons for the difficulties and caution students against reaching unsound solutions through seemingly easy methods.

MODERN WEIGHTS AND MEASURES. Two completely standardized systems of weights and spatial measures have been used in Japan since the Meiji period. One of these is the metric system, which has long been in general use among scientists and for official purposes, and which in 1959 was decreed to be the only system allowed for other common uses. The metric units seem already to have gone a long way toward complete public acceptance, and the day is probably not far distant when they will have entirely replaced the units of the other modern system.

The other system may be referred to as native, or Japanese. The names of the units in it are mostly of Chinese origin, but their values are not the same as those of the corresponding Chinese units. The native system has been standardized (i.e., defined in terms of the metric system) only since 1891, although rough definitions had been worked out about fifteen years earlier.

The native system contains units of the following kinds: weight; length or distance; cloth measure; area; and volume or capacity. Units of cloth measure refer to lengths of standard bolts. (There are various widths of standard bolts. The most common of them are approximately 36 cm., 70 cm., and 140 cm. The last-named width is used primarily for bolts of material used for Western-style clothing.) Cloth measures employ many of the same words as ordinary linear measures, but confusingly have values exactly one-quarter longer than the ordinary units of length.

There are numerous good sources for the correspondences between units of the Japanese system and those of the metric and English systems. These include special appendices to various editions of *Kenkyusha's New Japanese-English Dictionary*,[1] to Rose-Innes's *Beginner's Dictionary of Chinese-Japanese Characters and Compounds* (published in Tokyo in 1960), and Nelson's *Japanese-English Character Dictionary* (1962), as well as standard encyclopedias, historical encyclopedias, and statistical tables.

THE PREMODERN UNITS. When one comes to deal with units of measurement in use before the Meiji period the situation becomes complex indeed. The fact that the terminology used is roughly the same as that of the native system, fully standardized after 1891, may lead the uninitiated into believing that problems are as simple of solution as with modern units. Such is not the case. The intrinsic difficulty of the situation stems from three causes. First, at any given time there was not necessarily a standard definition throughout Japan of the value of any particular unit of measurement. Second, within the same area, the values of specific units did

---

[1] Senkichiro Katsumata, ed. (Tokyo, 1954).

not necessarily remain constant over long periods of time. Third, even with respect to different units of the same kind (e.g., units of weight, or of linear or volume measure) the ratios that existed at one time did not necessarily exist at another. Specific illustrations follow.

It is well known among modern students of measurements that there is a special value to be placed on the *ken* (the length of the standard architectural module—approximately six feet English linear measure) in certain parts of the Kansai region. That is, whereas the official definition of the *ken* makes it 1.82 meters, a common Kansai use of the same unit takes it to be 1.95 meters. A possible way of explaining the discrepancy is simply to say that that unit represents the unit of length which Japanese architects—in whatever part of Japan they may be—take as their basic measuring unit. The *ken* is thus the length of a *tatami*, or twice the width of one, or the distance between two successive vertical supports in a traditional building. It should be understood from this that the modular nature of Japanese architecture makes for uniformity in any locality in the values to be placed on the basic counting units used in constructing buildings. This does not mean, however, that the module was constant in different areas, and there is no assurance that even within the same general area there was absolute uniformity between the modules used by different artisans. The discrepancies among values assigned to other units of spatial measure and of weight were equally striking. In most cases measurement of particular objects was done by reference to instruments that were themselves unstandardized. That is, almost any manufacturer of foot rules, say, or of balance weights, could obtain from local authorities the right to define the exact dimensions of its own product.

It is to be expected that if the values of units varied considerably from place to place at any given time they were not even constant in a single place over long periods of time.

Variation might occur simply on account of gradual changes in dimension of the devices used for measuring, or they might occur because of sudden redefinitions of certain units. An instance of the imperceptibly slow kind of change is the fact that the standard *span* (distance between vertical supports) of Kamakura period buildings in the city of Kyoto, which was called one *ken*, does not exactly correspond to the *ken* unit used in the same city in the Tokugawa period. A famous example of the sudden kind of change was Hideyoshi's redefinition of the unit of area one *chō*, reducing it from 3,600 to 3,000 square *ken*. Hideyoshi is said to have effected this dramatic change in measure in order to raise the absolute amount of taxes collected on parcels of land without appearing to increase the amount levied on single measured units.

The last-named example shows that the ratios between different units of the same system did not necessarily remain constant over long periods of time. In fact at one and the same time there might be two or more sets of ratios in common use in different parts of the country. The *kin* is a unit of weight equivalent to 0.601 kg. and now contains 160 *momme* (1 *momme* = 3.759 g.). Before standardization, however, the same unit varied with the objects being weighed. It might be 160, 180, or 220 *momme*, the value of the *momme* being more or less constant.

Such were the confusions that existed before the Meiji period. The examples described should be enough to show that these problems are not for amateurs. Japanese specialists have done considerable work in tracing the history of each unit of measure, but understandably they have not been able to compile easy reference sources that will answer all questions involving measures at every place and time. There is a good historical study of linear measures in Japan by Fujita Motoharu.[2] There are also excellent brief definitions of the

[2] *Shakudo sōkō* (Tokyo, 1929).

principal premodern units of measurement in the historical encyclopedia *Nihon-shi jiten*. They are excellent because they are not more precise than the realities of premodern usages of the units warrant. It is also recommended that students consult the entries in general encyclopedias and historical encyclopedias (particularly the *Nihon rekishi dai jiten*[3]) under *hakari, doryōkō*, names of individual units, etc. Such modern scholarly aids will usually convey to the student what little firm information there is to be had on the subject.

MODERN MONETARY UNITS. The only common unit of Japanese currency today is the yen, exchangeable now (1964) and for the past several years at an official rate of 360 yen to one dollar. The *sen* (0.01 yen) remains a theoretical unit of monetary value, but since the wartime and postwar inflation it has ceased being a practical unit for coinage or pricing.

HISTORICAL PROBLEMS WITH MONETARY UNITS. The same caution applies to premodern monetary units as to premodern weights and spatial measures. In fact the system of measuring economic value was in some ways even more complex because Japan's primary medium of exchange and measure of wealth until well along in the Tokugawa period was not money at all, but bulk rice. Furthermore, money might be either metal or paper, and the former might be measured either as pieces with set values or by weight. Rates of exchange between rice and money sometimes fluctuated wildly, as did correspondences between different metals and between the piece and weight evaluations of coins of the same metal.

Meaningful conversions to present monetary units are impossible, and students are warned not even to attempt them. Nevertheless, certain other kinds of conversion are both fruitful and possible due primarily to the signal scholarly

[3] Kawade Takeo, ed. (20 vols.; Tokyo, 1956–60).

work in this field begun by the Japanese Finance Ministry over eighty-five years ago. From 1876 to 1883 the Ministry published the *Dai Nihon kahei-shi*, which has been revised and enlarged more recently,[4] and which is the most inclusive source for all kinds of information on the history of Japanese currency.

The main portion of this work consists of translations into modern literary Japanese of primary documents and other old sources. These are first placed into several broad classes, dealing with metal money, paper currency, local currencies, loans, trade, commodity prices, monetary exchange, and weights and measures. The sources within each of these sections are arranged chronologically. The editors have supplied numerous explanatory notes and illustrations. The raw material is here for systematic descriptions of comparative prices and values, but the material is hard to find because it is mostly in narrative rather than tabular form. Where it was possible for the editors to reduce all of the information on a certain matter to simple graphic terms they have done so, and the tables which the set includes are very valuable. One of them (volume 8, pages 83-89) shows the history of the national currency in the Tokugawa period, tabulating each new issue of a coin, the years during which it circulated, its weight, its gold or silver content, and the quantity minted. There are also tables showing commodity prices in different localities for selected dates in the 1870s (volume 6, pages 286-352).

A simplified table showing some of the same information as in the *Dai Nihon kahei-shi* appears in *Dokushi biyō*[5] (pages 743-73). Columns for selected dates from 1230 to 1825 show the value equivalences, where known, between unit volumes of rice, copper or gold pieces, and unit weights of silver. Certain

---

[4] Yoshida Kensuke, comp.; Honjō Eijirō, ed. (8 vols.; Tokyo, 1925–26).
[5] Tōkyō Teikoku Daigaku Shiryō Hensan-jo, comp. (Tokyo, 1933).

other monetary conversions (e.g., of local coinages in the Tokugawa period) appear in *Nihon-shi jiten* (pages 842-53).

CURRENT STATISTICAL SOURCES. Since the early Meiji period the Japanese government has been the leading agent for the compilation and publication of all kinds of statistics pertaining to Japan's economy and society. Most government agencies contain divisions specifically charged with keeping statistics, and a great many serial publications—monthly, quarterly, semiannual, and annual—are published under government auspices. These are the primary reference tools for researchers who need up-to-date statistical information or require very detailed statistics about any recent period.

There are two ways of approaching the problem of what specific publications to go to. One way is to consult a bibliography listing statistical sources to see what serials deal with the subject of one's inquiry and how frequently they are issued. There is a brief English-language guide in the University of Michigan's bibliographic series.[6] A more inclusive, but less recent, guide is that of Masaki Chifuyu and Matsukawa Shichirō;[7] and of course *Kanchō kankō-butsu sōgō mokuroku*, the official serial bibliography of government publications, lists statistical sources, but without annotations.

The other method of ascertaining what particular publication is best requires the use of the standard statistical index, *Nihon tōkei sō-sakuin*.[8] This is a subject index, arranged by similarity of topic and provided with a good table of contents. Each entry describes a single authoritative source of statistical information on the topic, giving the name of the governmental or private agency which compiled the information, a citation of the publication in which the information appears, and a

[6] Charles F. Remer and Saburo Kawai, *Japanese Economics: A Guide to Japanese Reference and Research Materials* (Ann Arbor, 1956).

[7] *Tōkei chōsa gaido bukku* (Tokyo, 1951).

[8] Semmon Tosho-kan Kyōgi-kai, comp. (Tokyo, 1959).

detailed description of the tables which the publication contains.

MODERN STATISTICAL COMPILATIONS. Students who use this index in any general library of Japanese reference materials will no doubt find that it refers them to many publications that are unavailable to them. In other words the publications indexed include some that can be found only in the largest deposit collections for government publications. Even those who do have access to the copious serial publications indexed here will frequently prefer to use a less cumbersome one-volume summary tabulation. The best known and most authoritative of these is the annual *Nihon tōkei nenkan* ("*Japan Statistical Yearbook*").[9] As the English subtitle indicates, this is a bilingual publication, using Arabic numerals and providing English translations for all column heads and explanatory notes. The coverage is very broad, embracing economic, demographic, social, and cultural matters. Though it is a current publication, aimed at keeping abreast of recent information, it incorporates statistics ranging back through several recent years in most of the tables which it contains. For the most important matters the work contains summary figures as far back as they are available.

The *Nihon tōkei nenkan* is a successor of a publication issued from 1882 to 1940 and known as *Dai Nihon Teikoku tōkei nenkan*.[10] For the years from 1940 to 1950, when the government brought out no equivalent works, consult the first issue (1950) of the postwar publication, which makes a special point of filling the gap in information.

Certain other reference books are worth mentioning for their statistical tabulations. Newspaper yearbooks, especially the *Nihon keizai tōkei-shū*,[11] *Meiji Taishō kokusei sōran*, and *Meiji*

[9] Sōrifu Tōkei-kyoku, comp. (Tokyo, from 1950).
[10] Naikaku Tōkei-kyoku, comp. (Tokyo, 1882–1941).
[11] Nihon Tōkei Kenkyū-jo, comp. (Tokyo, 1958).

Taishō zaisei shōran[12] are good one-volume summaries of the most important economic statistics ranging back to early Meiji.

Scholars who do considerable work with Japanese statistics have frequently complained about the imperfect proofreading standards that tend to mar certain Japanese statistical tabulations. Accuracy is the first requisite in any work consisting largely of figures, but such books are also notoriously difficult to make accurate. The authors know from personal experience that the newspaper yearbooks, which are produced under conditions of especially great haste, contain many typographical errors involving figures. The government publications and nonserial works mentioned above appear to be more reliable. Nevertheless, one should be cautious when one uses materials of this kind, where possible checking different sources of the same information against one another. Of course, if one finds that a column of figures does not add up to the total at the bottom of the column, it may mean simply that some of the figures have been rounded or that the column does not include all of the terms represented in the total. More frequently, however, a discrepancy between parts and sum is a clue that there has been a mistake.

[12] These last two compiled by Tōyō Keizai Shimpō-sha (Tokyo, 1929).

4. People and People's Names

THE PRESENT CHAPTER is concerned with problems relating to the identification and description of individuals. A word must suffice about that most irksome of all problems, recognizing a group of characters to be a person's name when one sees it in a Japanese text. Especially in *kambun* texts, inexperienced readers sometimes mistake names for common nouns, verbs, or dependent clauses, and one should be chastened by the example of the translator who rendered the name of a famous movie actress as *the 50 bells of Yamada*.

Other problems plague even the most experienced researchers. An individual may be known by a variety of names, and hence may be referred to in a document by a different name from the one he is listed under in a reference work. The pronunciation of his name may be unusual, perversely irregular, or even unknowable. Elementary information about a man's family, his education, his business or official connections, or his wealth or income may be indicated in a manner perfectly understandable to Japanese readers, but an enigma to others.

BIOGRAPHICAL DICTIONARIES. Two standard Japanese biographical dictionaries treat numerous famous people of all kinds, living and dead. They are *Dai jimmei jiten*[1] and *Dai Nihon jimmei jisho*.[2] The prewar edition of the former[3] is

---

[1] Heibon-sha, comp. (10 vols.; Tokyo, 1953–55).

[2] Dai Nihon Jimmei Jisho Kankō-kai, comp. (5 vols.; Tokyo, 1937).

[3] Heibon-sha, comp. [*Shinsen*] *Dai jimmei jiten* (9 vols.; Tokyo, 1937–41).

sufficiently different in point of view from its postwar revision so that students should know and use both of them.

There are also many books of the "Who's Who" variety, which treat prominent people alive at the time of preparation. Some of these fulfill much the same function as American credit registers, inasmuch as they indicate in one way or another an individual's wealth or income, in addition to giving vital facts of other kinds about him. Several English-language books with titles something like "Who's Who in Japan" have been prepared from time to time under various auspices, but naturally these are not so exhaustive as works of similar character in Japanese. Students should be aware of three in particular: *Jinji kōshin-roku* (begun in 1903), *Zen-Nihon shinshi-roku* (since 1950), and *Taishū jinji-roku* (since 1925).

There are also many dictionaries treating people distinguished in some special field or for some particular quality: Buddhist priests, Confucian scholars, living holders of Japanese copyrights, men currently in leading governmental positions, painters, members of the prewar nobility, etc.

Finally, one may refer to less obviously biographical reference works—general encyclopedias, annotated bibliographies like *Kokusho kaidai*,[4] and even linguistic dictionaries such as *Dai jiten* and *Dai Kan-Wa jiten*[5] (for famous Chinese and for Japanese Sinologists).

BIRTH AND DEATH DATES. Virtually all biographical reference works give dates of birth and death if they are known. They sometimes include wild guesses even if the dates are not known. The painter Kanō Masanobu is a case in point; various sources give birth dates for him ranging from 1434 to 1455, and death dates from 1492 to 1550. Such instances are fortunately rare, but they indicate that caution and skepticism are in order in one's own research. Check a

[4] Samura Hachirō, ed. (2 vols.; Tokyo, 1926).
[5] Morohashi Tetsuji, ed. (13 vols.; Tokyo, 1955–60).

number of reference works to be sure, and if there are discrepancies, attempt to find primary sources which may clear them up, or at least explain how they came about. Some large libraries maintain card catalogs called authority files, which record the variant dates found in different sources for a single individual. Librarians use these files to ensure accuracy and consistency in the information which appears with names of authors and subjects of book-length biographies on regular catalog cards. One common procedure among librarians is to regard as *established* any birth or death date if it appears in a certain number of works regarded as independent of each other. Students are warned, however, that the reference works cited above cannot be assumed to be *independent* sources merely because they are issued by different publishers. All of them may be based on the same earlier material, which may in some instances be erroneous.

Both birth and death dates are usually indicated in the familiar fashion, in parentheses after the name. Some biographical dictionaries, however, give the same information in a different way. They provide the death date in the body of the biography together with the man's age at the time of his death. If this method is used, remember that the age at death is most likely to be expressed in the Oriental manner, by which a person is regarded as one year old at birth and two at the beginning of the next calendar year. In other words, the age at any particular time is the number of different calendar years in which the man has lived. It is a larger figure by one or two than his age by Western calculation. To figure a man's year of birth from his year of death and age at death, convert the death year to its closest equivalent in the Western calendar (i.e., ignoring the overlap with the first part of the following Western year), add 1, and subtract the age at death. (For example, Tokugawa Mitsukuni died in the thirteenth year of Genroku, corresponding most closely to 1700 in the Western calendar. He was seventy-three at the time of his death. $1701 - 73 = 1628$. It makes no difference to this calculation that Mitsukuni died in the twelfth month of Genroku 13, and therefore in the early weeks of the Western year 1701. His age by Japanese reckoning remained the same during the entire civil year of the Japanese lunar calendar.)

Note that Japanese biographical dictionaries and other scholarly works that indicate years of birth and death according to the Christian era do not as a rule make the adjustment for dates at the end of the Japanese civil year. In other words, they would number as 1700 the entire civil year Genroku 13.

SURNAMES. Today Japanese possess both surnames and given names, and as in China the former always precede the latter both in speech and in writing. A man takes his surname from his *legal family*, usually the same as his blood or biological family, but not necessarily so, owing to the widespread custom of adoption. A married woman uses the surname of her husband.

In one form or another, surnames have existed in Japan since very early times, but until the nineteenth century they were privileges of aristocracy. In the earliest period they were perhaps more nearly akin to official titles or ranks of nobility than to family names as later Japanese have understood them. As titles and offices tended to be hereditary, names for them could, however, conveniently function as family names. Thus, the hereditary guild of armorers, *Mono no Be*, was also a *family*, identifiable by the same name. Other families of early Japan went by the names of localities in which they had been distinguished or with which they were otherwise identified. Here, as in the case of those indicating office or rank, names were granted officially by the imperial court. Thus, the family descended from the seventh-century statesman Nakatomi[6] no

---

[6] This was the name of a hereditary office.

Kamatari was granted the surname Fujiwara from the location of Kamatari's residence.

Aristocrats of the Nara and later periods usually appended to the name of their particular clan or family a title of rank known as *kabane*. Hence, the name of the ninth-century regent Fujiwara no Ason no Mototsune indicated that he was of the Fujiwara clan and held the rank of *Ason* 朝臣. In time, the whole designation Fujiwara no Ason came to be called a *kabane*, and finally the word *kabane*, written with the Chinese character for surname 姓, came to mean simply the name of a large aristocratic clan, such as Fujiwara. The bulk of the aristocracy of the Heian period belonged to four of these great clans, the Fujiwara, Minamoto, Taira, and Tachibana, which came to be known as the *shisei* 四姓—or four *kabane*.

Early surnames of the *kabane* variety were in official use among aristocrats until the nineteenth century, though there have been only a few historical figures since about the thirteenth century who have normally been identified by them. By that time members of the great clans had become so numerous and the family lines within clans so ramified that some means was needed of identifying individual branches of clans. Names of these subclans were originally informal or unofficial, but they are the true ancestors of modern Japanese surnames. Fujiwara nobles were identified by their families' residences in Kyoto wards like Konoe, Ichijō, and Sanjō, and those names later became the legal surnames of their descendants. Provincial nobility, whether of Fujiwara, Minamoto, or Taira ancestry, came to take as their family names those of the places where they lived or from which they derived their land revenues: Nitta, Ashikaga, Matsudaira, Tokugawa, and the like. Thus the redoutable ruler who signed himself in official documents as Minamoto no Ieyasu is known to history as Tokugawa Ieyasu, his subclan taking its name from a place where his ancestors had centuries before his time been land-holders.

The standard reference work on aristocratic surnames and genealogies, *Seishi kakei dai jiten*,[7] identifies the original clan from which each subclan claimed descent. When students encounter the converse problem, to determine the subclan name of an individual identified in a document by one of the four *kabane*, the most convenient source is the index volume of the *Kokushi takei* edition of *Kugyō bunin*.[8] Only holders of high titles conferred by the imperial court appear in this work, but these are the men whom one is most likely to find referred to in this way. If listed in the *Kugyō bunin*, a man's name appears in the index alphabetically by the *on* reading of the *personal name*, with clan and subclan names indicated.

In 1870, possession of a surname ceased to be an aristocratic privilege. Peasants and townsmen were required to take them, and most adopted names long in use among samurai or aristocratic families.

There were some other individuals in pre-Meiji Japan besides commoners who had no legal surnames and must be referred to by given name alone or by given name and title. Emperors, empresses, and those of their children who were not allowed to found families of their own had no surnames. The nomenclature used for them is of course complicated by the taboos surrounding all imperial things in Japan, but all the names which they possessed were of one or another of the classes of given names. Similarly, until the nineteenth century, Buddhist priests were considered to have "left their families," and are referred to by a special kind of Buddhist personal name known as *hōmyō* 法名—law name.

GIVEN NAMES. The most difficult thing about the given

---

[7] Ōta Akira, ed. (3 vols.; Tokyo, 1934–36).

[8] Kuroita Katsumi, ed., *Kugyō bunin* (5 vols.), in [*Shintei zōho*] *Kokushi taikei* (Tokyo, 1929–).

names of Japanese men is the fact that, particularly before the Meiji period, they tended to have so many of them. First, every adult man had a true personal name, his *na* 名 or *jitsumyō* 実名, which he usually chose for himself during his adolescence. This was the name by which he was known for all of the most official purposes. It was his personal property, so intimate in fact that other people tended not to use it at all, especially if its owner was an esteemed or powerful person. The *jitsumyō* of a ruler or father was actually taboo in ordinary speech for the man's subjects or children, and the *jitsumyō* of a venerated dead person was known as an *imina* 諱— literally an avoided name.

Typical given names of the *jitsumyō* class combine characters indicating desirable personal qualities, pronounced either by Sino-Japanese (*on*) or native Japanese (*kun*) readings, as Toshiaki, Yoshimitsu, and Kumbi.

The given name of boys too young to have acquired a *jitsumyō* was assigned by parents and called *yōmei* 幼名— childhood name. It had none of the taboo qualities of a man's *jitsumyō*, nor did the personal name of a woman.

The consequence of the peculiar notions about the *jitsumyō* of adult males in premodern Japanese society was that most of them had a variety of alternative given names for ordinary social purposes. One type served to identify the man among his family and close acquaintances, or in other words was similar in use to a man's first name in the West. It was called *tsūshō* 通称.

Tsūshō appear to have been little more than nicknames in their origins. Even superficially there is something commonplace and unofficial-looking about them. Some simply indicate the man's order of birth among the sons of his father: Ichirō, or Tarō—first son; Jirō—the next son; Saburō—third son; and so forth. There is surely nothing dignified enough to warrant taboos about these names.

Other *tsūshō* look like official or military titles: Gombei—provisional guard; or variants of *-uemon* or *-saemon*—right or left gate guardian. Such names may at one time have been true titles of office or rank, but in later Japanese history they were assigned to boys as half jocular nicknames, and in all cases are simply names, not real titles.

Well into the Meiji period most Japanese men had both true personal names and *tsūshō*, though the early Meiji government attempted to simplify things by having everyone settle on just one name both for official purposes and for common identification. The result was that from that time on more and more men limited themselves to just one ordinary personal name, but that name might be indiscriminately of the *jitsumyō* or the *tsūshō* variety. Among Meiji statesmen, Itō Hirobumi and Yamagata Aritomo employed their former *jitsumyō*, but Gotō Shōjirō used his former *tsūshō*.

Artists, teachers, scholars, and writers of pre-Meiji Japan usually had still other given names for professional purposes, for while the true name was too personal for common use, the *tsūshō* was likely to lack dignity. In imitation of Chinese practice, a scholar usually had a formal kind of name, called *ji* or *azana* 字, bestowed on him by his master or teacher. The equivalent among artists, actors, and so on was called *geimei* 芸名, a kind of studio name. In addition, scholars and writers in the Tokugawa period usually chose for themselves one or more pen names, known as *gō* 号. *Hōmyō*, the names of Buddhist priests, were analogous to laymen's given names of the *azana* or *gō* variety.

Finally, to complete this confusing picture, some individuals are referred to by completely unorthodox names. The woman who wrote *The Tale of Genji* is known as Murasaki Shikibu, since her regular name is unknown. Some modern writers and painters, and most stage and movie performers, adopt pseudonymous surnames, given names, or both, to protect the anonymity of their families or for reasons of glamour. (An interesting example is the writer of detective novels Edogawa Rampo, who assumed a pseudonym sounding as much as possible like Edgar Allan Poe.)

Most famous Japanese are known to history by just one of their several given names, but unfortunately there is no uniformity about the class of given name hit on for the purpose. Most political and military personages are known by their *jitsumyō* (e.g., Tokugawa *Ieyasu*), priests by *hōmyō* (Nichiren), and Confucian scholars by one or another of their *gō* (Arai *Hakuseki*), but in some exceptional cases the *tsūshō* may be the name to have lived in the history books (as with Yoshida *Torajirō*).

PROBLEMS OF IDENTIFICATION. As a scholar, you should identify people in as meaningful a way as possible. This means that you should always find the name by which Japanese historians refer to a man. If you find reference in an early eighteenth-century political document to Arai Kumbi, you should ascertain that the man in question is far better known by his *gō*, Hakuseki. Sometimes the most helpful procedure is to indicate to your readers the alternative given names by which a man may be identified in historical writing. The Confucian scholar Yoshida Shōin (a *gō*) is sufficiently often referred to in Western works as Yoshida Torajirō (his *tsūshō*) that a note to that effect is helpful if you mention him in your writings. Complete identification of a man sometimes requires that you give all of the names that he possessed.

Standard biographical dictionaries provide solutions to most of one's problems of identification and nomenclature. The name under which the biography of a man appears in the *Dai jimmei jiten* or *Dai Nihon jimmei jisho* is usually the one to use in your own references to him. Biographies in those works list alternative given names and say which class of given name they belong to. The indexes of those books list the alternative given names which one is likely to encounter most frequently. The index to *Dai Nihon jimmei jisho* is especially useful in finding the identity of a person who is referred to by an unusual alternative name, but see also the index to Mochizuki's *Bukkyō dai jiten*[9] for priests' names, *Nihon bijutsu jiten*[10] for names of artists, and *Nihon bungaku dai jiten*[11] for names of authors. Morohashi's *Dai Kan-Wa jiten* is particularly rich in *gō* of Confucian scholars, and the Heibon-sha *Dai jiten* is a mine of all kinds of information on nomenclature.

Names of modern Japanese are much easier to deal with, but even here caution is in order. Clarity requires that a writer be referred to by a penname (e.g., Natsume *Sōseki* instead of Kinnosuke, and Higuchi *Ichiyō* instead of Natsuko) if that is the way he would be recognized in a Japanese work. Here again, the biographical dictionaries (rather than "Who's Whos") offer the best guides.

A special problem of identification occurs in the case of Tokugawa-period political figures who held titles of court rank, usually ornamental, from the imperial court, and who were frequently referred to in contemporary documents by surnames and court titles (e.g., Oguri Kōzuke no Suke, whose title means Vice Governor of Kōzuke). Exceptionally, such a man may be commonly known by an abbreviated version of the court title (e.g., Oguri Kōzuke). Ordinarily, however, scholars must determine the man's *jitsumyō* in order to find out more about him in biographical sources. Standard biographical dictionaries give court titles of the people treated, but this is not very helpful if the surname is a common one, since the court titles do not appear in the indexes to these books. In addition, they include only the most famous of the thousands

---

[9] Mochizuki Shinkō, ed.; revised by Tsukamoto Zenryū (8 vols.; Tokyo, 1955–58). This work was originally published 1931–36.

[10] Noma Seiroku and Tani Nobukazu, ed. (Tokyo, 1952).

[11] Fujimura Tsukuru, ed. (8 vols.; Tokyo, 1951–52).

of officials of the Tokugawa period who possessed such titles. There are two more convenient places to look for names of people identified in this way. One of them is on pages 495-532 of *Dokushi biyō*, whose editors have indexed by court title all of the men listed in the great compendium of Tokugawa-period genealogy, *Kansei chōshū sho-kafu*, compiled in 1812. For names of individuals who lived after that date, it is recommended that students consult the *Dai bukan*,[12] a modern scholarly collection of the *bukan*, or rosters of feudal officials, compiled every few years by the Shogunate. Find the *bukan* nearest the date of your reference (a rough-and-ready procedure, and not infallible, but reliable enough if you are careful), and consult the roster of court titles that concludes the section.

PRONUNCIATION OF NAMES. There is still no Japanese publication which gives pronunciations of people's names in as convenient a fashion as in *Japanese Personal Names* and *Japanese Surnames* by Gillis and Pai.[13] *Seishi kakei dai jiten* is more authoritative on readings of surnames, but it lacks a character index, so one must make a guess in order to find a surname in the syllabic listing of the body of the book, if the reading of the name is irregular.

The reading of personal names is so troublesome that we can only recommend the same lighthearted attitude toward the problem that Japanese scholars themselves show. If you can find an attested reading of a man's name in a reference source, by all means use it, but if you cannot, find some plausible reading of the characters (asking native speakers of Japanese, if possible) and offer it as a modest suggestion. Note that even with modern given names the pronunciation used by the man himself is not necessarily the most recognizable. The Prime Minister from 1918 to 1921 apparently called

---

[12] Hashimoto Hiroshi, ed. (12 vols.; Tokyo, 1935–36).
[13] *Japanese Personal Names* (Peking, 1940); *Japanese Surnames* (Peking, 1939).

himself Hara Satoshi (and is so listed in *Dai jimmei jiten*), but he is much more famous either as Hara Takashi or as Hara Kei. All three possibilities are permissible readings of the same Chinese character.

OTHER BIOGRAPHICAL INFORMATION. The other facts about a man's life which one may find in biographical reference works require no such elaborate explanation. However, a few supplementary notes are in order for students requiring information of a kind not presented in a self-evident manner in the standard sources.

One may wish to know more about a man's ancestry or marital connections, for these are important in a culture that considers family lines as important as does Japan. Handbooks for historians, such as *Dokushi biyō* and Kyoto University's recent *Nihon-shi jiten* provide genealogies of the most prominent families, but do not necessarily indicate whether an individual belonged to his family by blood or adoption. *Seishi kakei dai jiten* gives information on family relationships, including genealogical tables showing heads of the most prominent families. A large body of genealogical literature from the past is incorporated in the anthology *Gunsho ruijū*,[14] including *Kōin jōun-roku*, which is the most authoritative source on the genealogy of the imperial family. Genealogies of daimyo and samurai families of the Tokugawa period, together with biographical information, appear in *Kansei chōshū sho-kafu*,[15] which is indexed in the modern scholarly edition. This monumental work (difficult to use because everyone in it appears under his true personal name, *jitsumyō*, rather than one that may be better known to historians) includes information about adoptive and marital relationships. Holders of prewar titles of nobility are shown in

---

[14] Hanawa Hokiichi, comp. [*Shinkō*] *Gunsho ruijū*; ed. by Ueda Mannen *et al.* (21 vols.; Tokyo, 1928–32).

[15] Yashiro Hirokata, comp.; ed. by Hotta Masaatsu (8 vols.; Tokyo, 1917–18).

the standard Japanese peerage, *Gendai kazoku fuyō*,[16] with genealogies.

"Genealogies" of a different kind, showing school affiliations of scholars, priests, and artists, contribute to one's knowledge of the development of artistic and philosophic traditions. Such may be found in *Dokushi biyō*, *Nihon keifu sōran*,[17] and specialized reference books on Buddhism, Confucianism, and the fine arts.

If one wants to know who held a certain office at a certain time, there are reference works for the purpose. *Kugyō bunin* shows yearly rosters of officials of the imperial court from the earliest times to 1868. The *Dai bukan* gives similar information for the Tokugawa Shogunate and *han* governments of the Tokugawa period, as well as for some other military governments of earlier times. *Shokuin-roku*,[18] published annually since 1886, is the best source on modern offices. For top personnel of companies and other nongovernmental organizations, see *Nihon shokuin-roku*.[19]

Modern works of the "Who's Who" variety give much information about people, including their wives and children, their publications (for which also see *Bunka jimmei-roku*),[20] their geographic origins and places of residence, the feudal connections of their families (in some instances), their education, and even their wealth. As these works have been much used by marriage brokers in arranging desirable matches, this last class of information has been considered essential. It usually takes the form of a single figure at the end of the biographical entry representing the number of yen of direct taxes paid by the individual during the year in question.

---

[16] Nihon Shiseki Kyōkai, comp. (Tokyo, 1929).

[17] Hioki Shōichi, comp. (Tokyo, 1936).

[18] (Tokyo, Ōkura-shō Insatsu-kyoku, from 1886). *Kan'in-roku,* a privately published roster, covers the period from 1868 to 1887, but it appears to be exceedingly rare in American collections.

[19] Jinji Kōshin-jo, comp. (Tokyo, from 1947).

[20] Nihon Chosaku-ken Kyōgi-kai, comp. (Tokyo, from 1951).

5. Problems of Geography and Place Names

A NUMBER of special difficulties beset the student of Japan who has a problem involving geographic information or place names. Names of places, like those of people, are likely to be irregular in reading. The system of official nomenclature, though orderly and precise, has changed from time to time in Japanese history, and even today administrative divisions change names on account of subdivision, amalgamation, or simply a desire for novelty. Students of early Japan must learn to cope with additional problems. They frequently deal with sources that reflect extremely primitive standards of cartography and geographic description. Even the topographic features of the country have changed greatly since the beginning of Japanese history: rivers have changed course, hills have been built up or worn away with human settlement, alluvial deposits have altered the coastline, and land use has worked further changes in almost all areas.

The geographic reference works that modern Japanese scholars have produced are very detailed and of a high standard of scholarly accuracy. Basic to all studies are maps, and the maps that the general student is likely to find easiest to use are those that appear in the various current atlases of modern Japan. Literally dozens of such books exist and new ones are published each year. Most of them include individual double-page maps of each prefecture as well as smaller scale maps of geographic regions and of the whole country. Customarily topographical and political features are superimposed on the same maps. Since the information contained is likely to vary little from one atlas to another, the choice of a particular title for one's reference use may as well be based on fringe benefits such as attractiveness of format or clarity of typography.

For greater detail and authenticity consult the separate sheets published by the official cartographic agency, the Chiri Chōsa-jo—Geographical Survey Institute—of the Construction Ministry. This body has mapped all of Japan at a scale of 1:50,000; another series of 1:25,000 maps covers most areas, and still more detailed maps exist for key regions. Some American libraries have good stocks of Geographical Survey Institute maps, and those still in print may be purchased directly from the agency. A catalog of maps and atlases currently useful, including some published by private bodies, may be found in Hall and Noh, *Japanese Geography: A Guide to Reference and Research Materials*, published in 1956 at Ann Arbor.

Historical atlases are indispensable for students of premodern Japan. Yoshida Tōgo's *Dai Nihon dokushi chizu* (Tokyo, 1939) is convenient and easily obtainable. The postwar *Nihon rekishi chizu*[1] supplements Yoshida's book with maps illustrating many topics of Japanese economic and social history, but the older work is still a better guide to the location of places mentioned in old-fashioned historical works that concentrate on details of political and military history.

Gazetteers, which are systematic compendia of verbal descriptions of localities, include much more detailed information than any map could possibly contain. One of these, in four volumes, *Nihon chimei jiten*, was published between 1954 and 1956 in Tokyo and may be regarded as the standard

---

[1] Nishioka Toranosuke and Hattori Shisō, eds. (Tokyo, 1956).

source on the topography, economy, and social and cultural life of places in contemporary Japan. Yoshida Tōgo's seven-volume *Dai Nihon chimei jisho* (1911-13) is still a standard source on historical geography because of its enormous detail and thorough documentation. However, the six-volume *Nihon chimei dai jiten* (1939), which incorporates much of the same information, is considerably easier to use because it is all in modern Japanese and its entries are arranged in kana order.

Not only do these gazetteers contain more information than historical atlases, but in some respects they are more accurate as well. In reading ancient history one may find references to places whose exact locations in terms of modern geography cannot be determined. For example, modern scholars may know of a certain village only that it lay in a certain province or somewhere on the bank of a certain river. A gazetteer will devote the necessary space to a description of the exact state of knowledge or ignorance that exists about such a locality, and it will probably specify as well the unproven theories current among scholars as to its location. An atlas, on the other hand, can only be definite and exact on such a point, sometimes more exact than the state of modern knowledge justifies.

KINDS OF PLACE NAMES. The first essential in identifying a place name is to determine what kind of geographic unit it refers to. Are the boundaries exactly defined (like those of New Jersey) or vaguely understood (as with the Middle West)? Is the place a feature of natural topography, such as a river, lake, mountain, or island? For purposes of scholarly description, a clear distinction should be made between units of the official system of geographic divisions that is used in the historical context of one's study, and unofficial or informal geographic units. Official place names usually have precise definitions and should be used precisely by scholars. Some such names refer to units of political administration. Others, such as names of streets or *chōme* in Japanese postal addresses, are merely convenient ways of describing a location and do not refer to administrative subdivisions.

Gazetteers of Japanese place names state or imply the class to which a given geographic unit belongs. The formal names of natural topographic features almost always include an element specifying the kind of feature, whether mountain, lake, river, or whatever. Up to this point Japanese practice is not much different from that in English (compare *Mt.* Fuji, *Lake* Biwa, etc.). Unlike English usage the formalities of written Japanese demand that a similar element appear in the names of most administrative and postal subdivisions as well. For example, the *city* of Nagasaki is formally referred to as Nagasaki-*shi* and the *prefecture* in which it is located as Nagasaki-*ken*. Things are less formal in speech, but even here there is a tendency for Japanese to use the class indicators as parts of official geographic names. So deeply ingrained has this habit become, in fact, that even those names that refer to vaguely defined regions (analogous to "Middle West") usually appear in Japanese followed by the word for region—*chihō* (e.g., Kantō *Chihō*; Chūgoku *Chihō*). Incidentally, the last example, which refers to the western peninsula of the island of Honshū, is thus clearly distinguished from the Japanese name for China, which is just Chūgoku. The principal exceptions to this rule that the formal names of places include inseparable class indicators are in the cases of foreign names; names of countries (including Japan); names of the largest islands of the Japanese archipelago (Honshū, Kyūshū, etc.); and the names of a number of streets or other postal subdivisions in rural areas, towns, and cities (e.g., Karasuma, a street in Kyoto; and Ginza and Jiyūgaoka, which are subdivisions of Tokyo wards).

The following description of the systems of official geographic nomenclature that have been in use at various times in Japan is written with the intention of making the descriptions in the gazetteers more meaningful.

PREMODERN SUBDIVISIONS. Although the system of local administration had undergone many changes before the Meiji Restoration, the system for naming localities had remained remarkably constant in its principal features for over a thousand years. The entire country was first of all divided into units known as *kuni* (written 国 or 州), usually translated as provinces. The exact number and boundaries of the *kuni* changed from time to time in ancient Japan, but by the Nara period most of these units had taken the names and denotations that they were to retain. In the early Meiji period, there were seventy-three of them, including the off-coastal islands of Sado, Oki, Iki, and Tsushima.

Within a *kuni* were units known as *kōri* or *gun* 郡, which one may translate district. Beneath the level of the *kōri* the named units were rural settlements that came eventually to be formalized as the *mura* 村—villages—and smaller units of Tokugawa and more recent times. Fortifications—*jō* 城—had distinctive names, as did market settlements—*machi* 町, or *shi* 市—though the names of these localities seem not to have been regarded as parts of any rationalized system for designating geographic areas.

From the period of the Taika Reform (A.D. seventh century) to the collapse of the imperial government system late in the Heian period (twelfth century) the names of the larger units in this system (*kuni* and *kōri*) corresponded to actual units of political administration. In addition there was another class of administrative units, the *dō* 道—circuits—to which one sometimes sees references in historical texts. There were seven of these, each containing several *kuni*, and they were originally the territories under the surveillance of imperial inspectors of provincial government. The seven *dō* together accounted for all of the territory of the realm except for the provinces

immediately surrounding the capital, which were known as
Kinai 畿内. The names of the seven *dō* were Tōkai-dō (the
Pacific seaboard extending eastward from the Kinai up to and
including the Kantō Plain); Tōsan-dō (the inland provinces
of central Honshū and the entire northeast portion of the
island); Hokuroku-dō (the Japan Sea coast from Wakasa Bay
to the Niigata Plain); San'yō-dō (the southern flank of the
Chūgoku Peninsula of western Honshū); San'in-dō (the
northern flank of the Chūgoku Peninsula); Saikai-dō (the
coastal portions of the Kii Peninsula directly south of the
Kinai, and the island of Shikoku); and Nankai-dō (Kyūshū).
Later the northernmost of the four great islands of the
Japanese group came to be referred to as an eighth circuit.
Its name, Hokkai-dō—or Northern Sea Circuit—has become
the official name of that island.

Even before the end of the Heian period, the actual government of provincial Japan had tended to fall outside the purview
of imperially appointed governors and into the hands of local
aristocracy. Thenceforth the most meaningful units of local
government were the domains of feudal rulers. These might
correspond roughly to *kuni* or *kōri*, but more often they did not.
Nevertheless, the *kuni* and *kōri* continued to be the only truly
systematic terms for purposes of geographic identification until
after the Meiji Restoration.

FEUDAL NOMENCLATURE. The atomization of political
control in the later Ashikaga period (fifteenth and sixteenth
centuries) created effective units of local administration that
had practically no relation to the units described above. These
were the domains of daimyos, almost independent feudal
rulers, and the subfiefs within them that belonged to daimyos'
vassals. Under the more centralized Tokugawa Shogunate the
former came to be the most important units of provincial
government and were called *han* 藩, and the subfiefs of rear
vassals tended to become mere fictions without true adminis-

trative functions. There were about 260 *han* at any one time in the Tokugawa period, in addition to the substantial area under the direct rule of the shogunate, which was known as the *tenryō* 天領. The *han* usually took their names from their castle towns or capitals. Thus, one usually refers to the Mito, Shizuoka, Saga, and Takamatsu Han. Certain very large feudal domains, embracing whole provinces or the larger part of provinces, were more frequently referred to by the name of the province (*kuni*) in which the castle town was located (e.g., Satsuma, Chōshū, Kaga, and Owari Han, which are less frequently identified by their castle towns of Kagoshima, Hagi, Kanazawa, and Nagoya, respectively). Note that the Satsuma Han was not coterminous with the *kuni* of Satsuma, nor were the other *han* so designated the same as the *kuni* for which they were named.

Tables showing the castle towns, ruling families, and assessed agricultural yield at various selected dates in the Tokugawa period may be found in several reference works, including *Dokushi biyō*, *Nihon-shi jiten*, and *Nihon rekishi dai jiten*. Unfortunately, there are no easy sources of information on the exact boundaries of the *han* at most dates. Maps showing the approximate boundaries of the *han* and the *tenryō* as of 1664 appear in *Nihon rekishi chizu*.

THE MODERN OFFICIAL SYSTEM. In 1873 the *han* were abolished and new units of local administration, known as *ken* 県, were established. The word was adopted from the usage of very early Japanese history when the *ken* or *agata* (same character) was a unit of provincial government subordinate to an imperially appointed governor. The *ken* in that sense was a precursor of the later *kōri*, and it is usually translated the same—district. In a modern context, however, the word *ken* is almost always translated as prefecture. Although the older *kuni* still continue to be used informally for geographic identification, the *ken* have replaced them for the most part as the largest units of local geographic nomenclature within Japan. There are now forty-two *ken*. Most of them were comprised of two or more *kuni*. More often than not the *ken* took their names from their capital cities.

On the same administrative level as the *ken* are four other units which are also normally called prefectures in English, since they are not much different in administration from the *ken*. One of them is Tōkyō-to, the metropolitan prefecture of Tokyo. Kyōto-fu and Osaka-fu are the prefectures containing those cities. Finally the island of Hokkaido is also a prefecture. Inasmuch as the terminal suffix *-dō* is itself an indicator of a class of subdivisions, no further suffix is ever appended to the name of Hokkaido to indicate its prefectural status. The generic name for the forty-six prefectures in Japan is *to-dō-fu-ken* 都道府県.

Territory within a prefecture is divided into urban and rural areas, known as *shi* 市—cities—and *gun* 郡—counties— respectively. Tōkyō-to is exceptional, for it contains the twenty-three wards, *ku* 区, of urban Tokyo as well as a number of *shi* and *gun*. Hokkaido contains a number of intermediate subdivisions known as *shichō*.

Subdivision in rural areas—*gun*—distinguishes between more and less heavily populated areas, *machi* 町—towns—and *mura* 村—villages—respectively. Both types of division are likely to contain areas of farm or forest land as well as settled communities.

Some smaller subdivisions in the system have administrative functions. One of them is the *ku* of large cities, which like the similarly named division in Tōkyō-to is an urban "ward." For the most part, however, they are purely conventional designations of larger or smaller areas and are used only for postal purposes. Within a *shi* are progressively smaller units known as the *chō* or *machi* 町, the *chōme* 丁目, and the *banchi* 番地. Within a *mura* are the *ōaza* 大字 and *aza* 字. Note that

none of the officially designated units of rural Japan correspond to our idea of a community, settlement, or village (though
the *ōaza* or *aza* may include only one such settlement). The
Japanese name for a single community in a rural area is *buraku*.
Most *mura* contain several *buraku*, which are important units
of economic and social life but have no essentially political
functions.

Note also that most city streets in Japan are named only
informally or unofficially, if at all. The streets of Kyoto are
exceptions, for they all bear names that one can find on maps
and that are known to the local citizenry. Some, but not all,
of these street names are even used for postal purposes.
However, the normal method of assigning postal addresses both
in cities and in the country is to specify the area, not the street,
in which the place is located. To the postman, Ginza in
downtown Tokyo is an area, not a street, though people
informally refer to the main street that runs through the
area by the same name.

The smallest unit of the postal system in cities, and in many
rural areas as well, is the *banchi*, an area bearing a number
rather than a name. The *banchi* are sometimes erroneously
referred to as house numbers. Some of them contain only one
house and some contain none at all, but most of them contain
a great many, especially in districts which have become more
densely populated since the *banchi* numbers were assigned. The
arrangement of *banchi* within a *chō*, *chōme*, or *aza* in some cases
proceeds according to no discernible order. That is, *banchi*
number 5 of an area may be adjacent to number 6, but then
again it may not.

The general scheme for subdividing Japan into areas for
administrative or postal purposes is shown in the accompanying
figure.

The administrative system undergoes continuous changes in
detail, and names of administrative units sometimes change.

Two of the reference works which record in tabular form the principal changes that have occurred in Japanese history are *Nihon-shi jiten* (pages 548–578) and *Dokushi biyō* (pages 551–610). For other changes, see the descriptions under individual place names in *Nihon chimei dai jiten*.

IDENTIFICATION OF HISTORICAL PLACES. The foregoing discussion should make it clear that the most accurate and meaningful way of identifying a place to which one finds reference in a historical source is in terms of present-day official subdivisions or of physical landmarks. Though the prefectural system adopted in early Meiji has considerably changed the official terminology on the provincial level, names

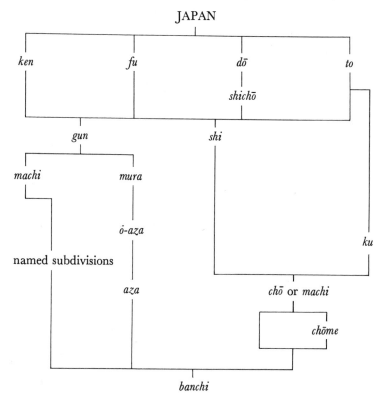

of smaller units are often remarkably similar to those in use centuries ago. When one reads a description in a historical gazetteer of a historical site, one can then use the maps in a modern atlas to visualize the location in reference to modern physical or political geography. Thus the site of Oda Nobunaga's castle at Azuchi might be described either as "in present-day Azuchi-mura, Gamō-gun, Shiga-ken" or "on a promontory on the eastern shore of Lake Biwa, about thirty kilometers northeast of Ōtsu."

PRONUNCIATION OF PLACE NAMES. If one knows the location of a place one can find the currently accepted pronunciation of the name in one of the gazetteers of place names published to accompany modern atlases. The arrangement in these works is first by prefectures, and within each prefecture by successively smaller units of the system. A number of place name dictionaries have been published specifically for the purpose of giving standard readings of names currently used. The best would appear to be that recently prepared by the Japan Broadcasting Company (*NHK*) for the information of its announcers and others under the title *Nihon chimei hatsuon jiten*.[2]

There is not the same degree of scholarly standardization for historical place names no longer current. Foreign scholars are well advised to adopt the readings suggested in the main alphabetic listing of the *Nihon chimei dai jiten* or the alphabetic index of the *Dai Nihon chimei jisho*. The latter is supplied with a separate character index for irregularly pronounced names. The Heibon-sha *Dai jiten*, Morohashi's *Dai Kan-Wa jiten*, and other linguistic dictionaries and general encyclopedias are also useful sources on place name pronunciation.

SOURCES FOR HISTORICAL GEOGRAPHY. Historical writings abound in facts about localities that may be of importance

---

[2] (To be 8 vols.; Tokyo, from 1959).

to scholars of historical geography. Most are found in works whose authors did not conceive of themselves as recording geographic information. Novels, poems, formal works of history, and essays on almost any subject may embody unique pieces of knowledge about places and their names. Much of the information incorporated in the modern gazetteer *Dai Nihon chimei jisho* was known to its compiler through his vast learning in formal and informal written works.

There are also early geographic reference works of a more systematic sort. One class of these is known as *chishi* 地誌, a premodern precursor of the gazetteer. The earliest of these were the *Fudo-ki*—Topographic Records—compiled by imperial order in the eighth century to describe the features of natural and historical geography of every province. Only five of these are fully extant, but fragments of others remain embedded in later historical works, and will help to illuminate for us the circumstances of provincial life in Japan of the Nara period.

One great compilation of premodern geographic information is the "Kokugun-shi," or "Essay on Provinces and Districts" of the *Dai Nihon shi*,[3] compiled in the nineteenth century but dealing with Japan as it was in the fourteenth and earlier centuries. Another source is the geographic section of the Chinese-style encyclopedia *Koji ruien*.[4]

[3] (17 vols.; Tokyo, 1928–29), vol. XV.
[4] (60 vols.; Tokyo, 1931–36), vols. III-V.

6. Words and Their Meanings

BASIC to all reading in foreign languages is the problem of finding accurate definitions of words. It goes without saying that the reader should have in his head the definitions of the most common words and should know how to look the others up. Nevertheless, no native to the English language has ever read a Japanese text accurately or translated one satisfactorily by means of dictionary definitions alone. Even when dealing with a language closely related to English, one must have a highly developed sense of the style and flavor peculiar to that language in order to do these things well. The difficulties are compounded many times over in handling a language as different from our own as Japanese. Some words correspond exactly to English equivalents, but most do not. *Seishin* does not really mean "spirit" but that is about the best definition the dictionaries are able to provide. Philosophers of semantics might even question whether *uma*, which really does mean horse, has quite the same connotations of horsiness as the English word. Everyone knows that idioms are "untranslatable," but everyone agrees they should be translated.

But the most important reason that mechanical renderings of Japanese words do not always produce good English equivalents is simply that the Japanese have different experiences from ours and consequently have different habits of expression. They say things that we would not say, or say them in ways that we would not. "*Tadaima!*" is the greeting that all Japanese would call upon entering their own houses. Literally it means "now," and its semantic equivalent is something like "I'm back now." Nevertheless, in the Western world the closest social equivalent is silence. The troublesome word *daihyō-teki* illustrates a combination of these difficulties. The dictionary definition is "representative," but it is clear from the way in which it is used that it has no sense of typicality or averageness. In fact, where a Japanese would call Beethoven's Fifth Symphony *daihyō-teki*, we would probably say that it is one of the best.

GENERAL PROBLEMS OF TRANSLATION. It can be seen that it is not enough to find an unknown word in a dictionary and fit its definition into the sentence at hand. Examples of the context in which a definition is or was used should be studied to see if it applies to the immediate question and to gain a deeper feeling for the word that will help one to interpret it when one sees it again.

Translation presupposes a thorough knowledge of the historical and social background of the original text. A definition current now is almost certainly different from the one in use three hundred years ago. Languages are dynamic. They change with each generation. A major social upheaval like war or revolution causes profound changes in vocabulary and usage. If it results in a realignment of social classes, the entire grammatical structure of the language may change perceptibly. Contact with foreign countries, or the lack of it, or the growth of technology or material culture deeply influences vocabulary and the development of style.

Let us assume, however, that the writer of the original Japanese text is one of our own contemporaries, that he is an educated man and a skillful user of words, and that therefore the historical context is not much of a problem. The translator aims as always to produce the closest English approximation of the sense and other values of the original text, but he is instantly faced with a problem. Those other values, which may include naturalness of diction, psychological nuance, or literary beauty, do not always survive the transference to another language of the strict sense and manner of expression of the original.

The purpose for which the original was written may help to determine what standards of exactitude or of literary merit should apply to one's translation. At one extreme are works of pure science, which are customarily written in pure prose, and in which *sense* is the all-important thing. Literary frills would be wasted on them, but of course economy and clarity of style would not. At the other extreme are works of *belles lettres*, in which the word-for-word meaning of the original is less important than the complex of denotations and connotations conveyed by the whole.

Obviously, one absolute prerequisite for translating the literature of a foreign language is the ability to write one's own language with sensitivity and skill. The translator who lacks it will not only produce an ugly translation but one which is likely to be misleading or inaccurate as well. The translator in some ways has a greater responsibility to his readers than that of a creative author. Of course he must convey the meaning and intention of the original author, but he must also do it as gracefully as his skill permits. If he translates a three-word expression, for instance, into a compound sentence with several relative clauses, he may mislead his readers more than if he had not translated the expression at all. A brief study of some of the translations from Japanese literature, still, alas, available to the public, will reveal the horrors which can result when a poor writer handles a foreign language he does not understand very well written by a people he comprehends even less. The obligation to translate in a good literary style applies not only to specialists in pure literature; it is mandatory for most other scholars as well. To translate into stilted, garbled English is to convey to the unsuspecting reader a conception that the original work was, at the very least, dull and plodding, and a strong suspicion that its author was deficient in talent and imagination.[1]

The practicing scholar must constantly try to increase his knowledge of the Japanese language through broad reading. The insight which will enable him to leap from the denotation of words or phrases to the true meaning inherent in the text cannot be acquired in any other way. Only when he has attained some degree of proficiency in reading Japanese will he be able to transpose it skillfully into English.

Dictionaries are the most indispensable tool of the scholar. By choosing judiciously those which he uses, he may solve problems of vocabulary and usage accurately and expeditiously. As a general rule, a dictionary that attempts to describe how the meaning of a word or phrase has changed throughout the years is better than one that offers only one set of current definitions for each entry. If it is possible to use a dictionary written expressly to analyze the language of a given period (its own, or another in the past) the same purpose is served. It is advisable, therefore, at an early stage in one's research, to survey the dictionaries available and determine which are most likely to contain definitions appropriate to the material under study.[2] Even when the title fails to describe which period or periods in history were most carefully studied in the preparation of the book, reading of the preface or some small amount of investigation into the specialties of the editors will

---

[1] The best way to study the techniques of translating is to read some of the finer examples available; for instance, Arthur Waley's *The Tale of Genji* by Murasaki Shikibu (2 vols.; New York, 1935), Donald Keene's *The Setting Sun* by Dazai Osamu (Norfolk, Conn., 1956), or Edward G. Seidensticker's *The Makioka Sisters* by Tanizaki Junichirō (New York, 1957).

[2] A survey of the history of dictionaries in Japan and an annotated bibliography of them can be found in Joseph K. Yamagiwa, *Japanese Language Studies in the Shōwa Period*, 32–50.

often help you to measure its usefulness to you in your own work.

There are two broad classes of dictionaries of Japanese—those indexed by characters and those arranged according to the kana syllabary or other phonetic system. There are some differences in coverage and function between the two besides the obvious ones, and a student would do well to know which type is more likely to answer his needs in particular cases. Experience has shown that as between two dictionaries of comparable size the character dictionary is likely to be the more authoritative for reading *kambun*, works on Buddhism or philosophy, and, in general, texts by Japanese whose education belonged to the classic Confucian tradition. The phonetic dictionary, on the other hand, would tend to be better for works of Japanese literature, modern scientific and technological works, and most other texts dating from the modern period.

Both kinds of dictionaries contain definitions, and in addition the largest and best works of both classes include examples of the way in which words, characters, morphemes, or particles have been used in different periods. Japanese dictionaries rarely specify the dates of the quoted examples, but they mostly arrange them in chronological order and indicate by title the work from which an example was taken.

CHARACTER MEANINGS AND ETYMOLOGIES. To find the meaning, reading, and history of an unknown character one must use a character dictionary. To learn the shades of distinction that may have been implied by the choice of one character over another to represent a certain Japanese word, a character dictionary is again in order. Still another function which only that sort of book will serve is to show by quoted examples from *Chinese* texts the classic usages that have helped to shape Japanese writers' use of characters. It will be noticed that the huge majority of examples in character dictionaries are from Chinese classical literature or from works in Chinese (*kambun*) by Japanese writers. This is attributable to the fundamental feature of these works, that they aim to convey information about Chinese characters rather than about Japanese words. A student who has even rudimentary knowledge of Chinese can gain the greatest usefulness from character dictionaries, for he can refer to the text from which an example was chosen to enhance his understanding of the character. The better dictionaries of this sort also attempt to note any differences between the way a character is used in Chinese and the meaning it took on during the years in Japan.

When it appears that the classical definition does not apply to your own problem and no further explanation is offered in a character dictionary, it is necessary to consult a dictionary arranged phonetically. Similarly, when the compound you seek is not listed, you must combine plausible readings of the separate characters and proceed to the other sort of dictionary. Should this technique fail, an educated guess based on the meanings of the individual characters may very well produce as good an answer as you can hope to find.

For the novice, there are two good bilingual character dictionaries, Arthur Rose-Innes's *Beginners' Dictionary of Chinese-Japanese Characters* and Andrew Nathaniel Nelson's *The Modern Reader's Japanese-English Character Dictionary*. The latter is larger and better for strictly current materials, but Rose-Innes's book includes some literary expressions and words no longer completely current that have been left out of the later work. Even for students at the early stages of study, the brevity of the definitions in these two books makes it necessary to use them in conjunction with a larger dictionary like *Kenkyusha's New Japanese-English Dictionary*.[3]

---

[3] For prewar studies the older edition edited by Takenobu Yoshitaro is recommended (American edition; Cambridge, 1942).

For students of the Meiji period, F. Brinkley's *An Unabridged Japanese-English Dictionary* (Tokyo, 1896) will be found to be very useful.

While the systems of arrangement invented by Rose-Innes and Nelson enable the student to locate characters in these books with relative ease, they also act as a handicap when he attempts to use dictionaries compiled by Japanese scholars. To avoid undue future dependence on bilingual dictionaries and to increase one's confidence in Japanese, it is advisable to turn to a simple dictionary like the *Tōyō kanji jiten*[4] at an early stage. This work is suitable only for reading contemporary materials, and as his ability to handle Japanese increases a little, the student will want to go on to a more comprehensive dictionary. The recently revised *Kan-Wa chū jiten*[5] seems admirably well suited to fill this role. Compiled by three eminent sinologists, it was designed to assist in reading both classical and modern texts. The definitions are in clear, concise modern Japanese and avoid the lexicographic pitfall of explaining words in terms of themselves. These two desirable attributes are unfortunately lacking in Ueda Mannen's famous *Dai jiten*, published in 1940.

The most exhaustive character dictionary extant is the *Dai Kan-Wa jiten* by the great sinologist Morohashi Tetsuji. The whole range of possible meanings, common and obscure, ancient and modern, is described for each character. The compounds listed include people's names, place names, titles of books and essays of all kinds, and literary expressions, as well as common nouns. Many of the entries are so extensive as to be full-scale encyclopedia articles. All *kambun* texts are punctuated. There is no better place to go for assistance in reading the Chinese classics, Chinese texts written in Japan, and Japanese language materials with problems related to characters.

The *Dai Kan-Wa jiten* does not attempt to exhaust the field

[4] Seki Kan'ichi and Tomiyama Tamizō, comp. [*Katei-ban*] *Tōyō kanji jiten* (rev. ed.; Tokyo, 1961).

[5] Kaizuka Shigeki *et al.*, comps. [*Kadokawa*] *Kan-Wa chū jiten* (Tokyo, 1959).

of Buddhist vocabulary. For that the student may turn to Oda Takunō's excellent one-volume dictionary,[6] originally compiled in 1917, or to Mochizuki Shinkō's encyclopedic work,[7] of somewhat later date. Both of these contain biographical, philosophic, and geographic information as well as definitions of words and phrases. *A Dictionary of Buddhist Terms*, compiled by Soothill and Hodous and published in London in 1937, is the best bilingual dictionary in this field.

JAPANESE WORDS AND THEIR ETYMOLOGIES. There are a great many small- and medium-sized dictionaries of the Japanese language arranged according to the syllabary. Almost any of these will serve adequately for ordinary purposes but advanced research requires the use of a larger, more comprehensive set. As a general tool for the scholar, nothing is better than the *Dai jiten* published by Heibon-sha. It contains ordinary words, noting in many cases changes that have occurred throughout the centuries and citing literary references; both literary and colloquial phrases and expressions; regional variants of standard words and words existing only in dialects; grammatical elements like postpositional particles, verb endings, and conjunctions; and brief descriptions of a great many people, places, and books.

Its great size (26 volumes) is its best feature. The order of arrangement is simple and obvious, and the definitions are, generally speaking, readily comprehensible. For all its vast coverage, the *Dai jiten* is not without it deficiencies. There are occasions when the reader finds himself in the frustrating situation of seeing a word defined in terms of another word which does not itself appear in the dictionary. In other instances, comprehension of the definition depends upon understanding a dense quotation, whereupon it is necessary

[6] [*Oda*] *Bukkyō dai jiten* (rev. ed.; Tokyo, 1954).
[7] See page 50.

to go to an annotated edition of the original source in the often vain hope of gaining further insight. The examples themselves are at times inaccurately quoted and must therefore be checked before they can be used.

The *Dai genkai*[8] by Ōtsuki Fumihiko enjoys a higher reputation among scholars than the *Dai jiten*. Ōtsuki was one of the first etymologists in Japan and his book is the fullest source of information on etymologies of Japanese words. The *Dai genkai* is a revised and expanded version of a dictionary he completed in 1884 and as such is particularly rich in words in use in the early Meiji period. Although the definitions are often extremely difficult to understand, there are many examples quoted for words whose meanings have changed over the years, and the effort required to understand the quotations can generally be justified in terms of the additional information obtained.

There are two other excellent dictionaries of a size comparable to the *Dai genkai*. One is *Kotoba no izumi*[9] and the other is *Dai Nihon kokugo jiten*.[10] All three of these works suffer from the fault of defining words in terms of themselves.

There exist many specialized dictionaries, most of them only one volume in length. In addition to technical and scientific dictionaries, one may wish to become familiar with those dealing with the ancient classical language; argot; dialects of certain areas or periods; foreign words in use in Japan; the terminology used in fine arts, or some branch of the theatrical arts, or applied arts and crafts. Unfortunately, these small dictionaries are rarely as rewarding as their respective titles would seem to indicate, and all too often they do not contain many more entries in their field than the large, inclusive sets. On the other hand, the definitions offered are based on the

---

[8] (4 vols. plus index; Tokyo, 1932–37).

[9] Ochiai Naobumi, comp. (5 vols. plus index; Tokyo, 1929).

[10] Ueda Mannen and Matsui Kanji, comp. [*Shūtei*] *Dai Nihon kokugo jiten* (Tokyo, 1958).

results of concentrated research in a particular area, and they therefore cannot be disregarded.

WORDS THAT ARE NOT IN DICTIONARIES. The search for an adequate definition of a word will often lead the student far from so obvious a source as a linguistic dictionary. The word may not appear in any dictionary. It may appear with definitions that are clearly inapplicable. Imagination and erudition are one's best resources in such a case. It is wise to consider the following possibilities.

The word may be a proper noun. Would a personal or place name make sense in the context? Could it be the name of a Chinese; or of a Western city or country written in Chinese characters chosen to represent the sound? A brand name or name of a commercial establishment?

The word may be a typographical error. Does one of the characters look like some other that would make better sense? Would it help to substitute one kana for another? Would it improve matters if the characters of a compound were reversed?

The original writer may have made a mistake in orthography or character choice. Errors may be illiterate or merely imaginative (e.g., 左右です Sō desu: Natsume Sōseki). The use of okuri-gana (the kana following a Chinese character that indicate which of several possible words or grammatical forms of a word the character is intended to represent) has varied among writers of skill and education. Sometimes a writer may represent a Japanese word with a Chinese character of related meaning which no dictionary lists as an accepted way of writing that word.

The word may be a joke. The punning possibilities of the Japanese writing system are infinite, and Japanese writers like plays on characters and words. The form 六ケしい—for muzuka-shii—was probably once a kind of pun.

If the text is very recent it may contain new coinages that have not yet found their way into dictionaries. Regardless of the date of the text it may contain expressions too ephemeral to have been recorded elsewhere.

CLASSICAL AND LITERARY ALLUSIONS. The surface meaning of an expression may be clear but still make no sense in the context. In such cases one should consider whether the expression might be an allusion to some earlier literary work or to a saying, custom, or historical event remembered by the readers for whom the text was written. There are two categories of reference works that may be useful in tracing down allusions: studies of classical literature and books dealing systematically with aspects of Japanese ethnography such as manners and customs, religious practices, food, dress, household furnishings, and proverbs and sayings.

The great monuments of Japanese literature have been exhaustively studied and are constantly being reevaluated. Concordances to the words appearing in these famous texts will not offer any definitions, but they will tell you where the words occur in the text. By studying several examples with the help of glosses, you will be able to gain some understanding of their meaning. A concordance is useful, then, not only in reading the classic itself but in the study of other material of the same period or of a later date, particularly if it can be determined that the author of the work at hand has himself been influenced by that classic. The metaphors, images, phrases, and symbols of the early collections of Japanese poetry, for instance, have been used over and over thousands of times throughout the centuries. Knowledge of their original meaning is almost essential to the comprehension of later poetry, plays, and even popular fiction. A concordance is often published as part of a large study of the work to accompany an authoritative or variorum edition of the text, as in the case of the *Man'yō-shū taisei*[11] and *Genji monogatari taisei*.[12] It may also

[11] (22 vols.; Tokyo, 1953–56).
[12] Ikeda Kikan, comp. (8 vols.; Tokyo, 1953–56).

be issued as a separate volume with the title *sō-sakuin*, as the *Kokin-shū sō-sakuin*.[13]

Words appearing in the classics which offer particularly vexatious problems or are of great philological interest may be the subject of whole articles or even books. These studies are usually far too specialized to be of immediate use to the scholar whose field is not literature, but anyone who is making a thorough study of the text or of historical documents of a very early date will need to be aware of them. There are several journals specializing in philological studies, among them *Kokugo kokubun*, issued by Kyoto University, and *Kokugo to kokubungaku*, compiled at Tokyo University.

Special dictionaries have been compiled which deal exclusively with the language and grammar of the classics or with the vocabulary appearing in the texts of one author. As in the case of the concordances, they often can be used in reading works other than those for which they were designed. A work like the *Genji monogatari jiten*[14] can function as a dictionary of Heian period Japanese and the *Chikamatsu goi*[15] as a guide to the vast body of theatrical literature influenced by that playwright.

When reading diaries and journals, novels, and plays one frequently encounters casual reference to the social habits that make up the daily life of the Japanese people. They are often of such an obvious nature that no native lexicographer would consider them worthy of mention, but to the foreign student they are as puzzling as the most obscure reference to the Chinese classics. Information relating to such problems can be found in the *Nihon shakai minzoku jiten*.[16] Here, under broad general topics, are detailed descriptions of, for instance, articles of clothing, holidays, legends, and ceremonies peculiar

---

[13] Nishishita Kyōichi and Takizawa Sadao, comps. (Tokyo, 1958).
[14] Kitayama Keita, comp. (Tokyo, 1957).
[15] Ueda Mannen and Higuchi Yoshichiyo, comps. (Tokyo, 1930).
[16] Nihon Minzoku-gaku Kyōkai, comp. (4 vols.; Tokyo, 1954–60).

to certain regions. Unusual expressions and habits of speech
are also considered, but for these a compendium like the
Sōgō Nihon minzoku goi[17] is usually a better source. For proverbs,
the *Gengo dai jiten*[18] appears to be the most inclusive work
available.

As in every other type of research, the kind of problem
will dictate the choice of reference material. Once you have
determined the general category in which the word you seek
belongs, scanning an essay in a general encyclopedia on that
broad subject may reveal the definition you need. A collection
of sources which contains material on manners and customs like
the *Meiji bunka zenshū*[19] or the *Koji ruien* is often helpful, as
are contemporary newspapers and special studies of the society
of a given period.

[17] Minzoku-gaku Kenkyū-jo, comp. (5 vols.; Tokyo, 1955–56).
[18] Fujii Otoo, comp. (Tokyo, 1926).
[19] Yoshino Sakuzō, ed. and comp. (24 vols.; Tokyo, 1928–30).

7. General Problems Concerning Written Sources

THE PROBLEM of ascertaining what written materials exist for the study of a subject is basic to all scholarly work, and as such it has been discussed in Chapter 1. In this and the following chapters we shall treat the problems that occur to a student who has already found his bearings in the basic sources for his subject, but would like to know what use he can make of them.

Here we deal with some elementary questions about written sources that can usually be handled simply provided that the student has access to an adequate collection of Japanese reference books: Who wrote the book and when? How should the title be pronounced? What sort of book is it, and what, in general, does it contain? What are the judgments of other scholars as to its value? Where can a copy of it be found? These questions must be answered before going on to the more complex problem, dealt with in subsequent chapters of this book, of evaluating the accuracy of a written source and determining its usefulness for one's own purposes.

ANNOTATED BIBLIOGRAPHIES AND THEIR USE. There is an important class of Japanese annotated bibliographies which contain information of a general kind about books and other written materials. These are called *kaidai* 解題, and are similar to other types of annotated bibliographies except that they customarily give more detailed information. Their coverage tends to be more nearly exhaustive as regards premodern materials, before, say, the Meiji Restoration.

The grandparents of the form are two works of the late Tokugawa and early Meiji periods, *Gunsho ichiran*[1] and *Kokusho kaidai*. Both consist of their editors' reading notes on a great many historical, literary, philosophic, and religious works. Two modern works are similar in coverage, but are of course based on more recent scholarship and describe some modern books. These are *Shiseki kaidai*[2] and its successor, by some of the same editors, *Kokushi bunken kaisetsu*.[3]

Kanseki kaidai[4] contains similar information for premodern books written in China. For Buddhist works—including those from mainland Asia—one should consult the *Bussho kaisetsu dai jiten*[5] or the descriptive sections of *Shōwa hōbō sō-mokuroku*.[6] The latter is the index supplement prepared to accompany the *Taishō shinshū Daizōkyō*,[7] the great Japanese scholarly edition of the Chinese Buddhist canon, which includes many works by Japanese Buddhists as well. As one additional example of specialized works of this kind, see [*Sakoku jidai*] *Nihonjin no kaigai chishiki*,[8] whose title does not indicate that it is a *kaidai* of Tokugawa period works dealing with foreign countries.

Similar descriptions of written sources may be found in other, less obvious, books. Modern editions of Japanese literary classics, works of history, and other important sources on the past frequently include critical introductions, in which the

---

[1] Ozaki Masayoshi, comp.; Irita Seizō, ed. (Tokyo, 1931). Continued in Nishimura Kanebumi, comp.; Irita Seizō, ed., *Zoku gunsho ichiran* (Tokyo, 1927).

[2] Endō Motoo *et al.*, eds. (Tokyo, 1936).

[3] Endō Motoo and Shimomura Fujio, eds. (Tokyo, 1957).

[4] Katsura Koson, ed. (Tokyo, 1922).

[5] Ono Gemmyō, comp. (12 vols.; Tokyo, 1933–36).

[6] Takakusu Junjirō and Watanabe Kaigyoku, eds. (3 vols.; Tokyo, 1929–34).

[7] Takakusu Junjirō and Watanabe Kaigyoku, eds. (85 vols.; Tokyo, 1914–32).

[8] Kaikoku Hyakunen Kinen Bunka Jigyō-kai, ed. (Tokyo, 1953).

nature and importance of the work, its authorship, textual history, and other pertinent matters concerning it are discussed. One recent set of standard literary classics[9] contains introductions of this kind for all of the works included, as do several of the major anthologies, *sōsho*, which are the most convenient places to look for the shorter works from premodern Japan.[10]

Students of pre-Meiji history would do well to be familiar with two essays by modern historians in which the most important features of a great many historical sources are described. One of these is the chapter on Japan's main historiographical tradition in the introductory volume of Kuroita Katsumi's *Kokushi no kenkyū*.[11] The other is the excellently indexed three-volume guide by Kurita Motoji, *Sōgō kokushi kenkyū*.

General encyclopedias and even the larger linguistic dictionaries may be of help in providing information about the most important books, and one should not overlook specialized encyclopedias for descriptions of works in the fields to which they pertain. Fujimura's *Nihon bungaku dai jiten*, for example, contains synopses, descriptions, and appraisals of works of literature, premodern and modern. The *Nihon rekishi dai jiten*, the most comprehensive general encyclopedia of Japanese history published to date, describes historical sources, formal histories, and essays on historical subjects.

The above reference books deal with no more than a small fraction of the significant books which have been published since the Meiji Restoration. The best annotated bibliography of modern scholarly materials on history and related disciplines

[9] Iwanami Shoten, ed., *Nihon koten bungaku taikei* (Tokyo, 1957–).

[10] See in particular Hanawa Hokiichi, comp.; Ueda Mannen, ed. [*Shinkō*] *Gunsho ruijū* (21 vols.; Tokyo, 1928–32).

[11] (Tokyo, 3rd rev. ed., 1931), pp. 155–211.

is the series prepared under the editorship of Honjō Eijirō.[12] The bibliographical essays formerly published by the Rekishi-gaku Kenkyū-kai[13] also provide a certain amount of similar information on current publications.

TITLES OF BOOKS. To romanize the title of a book, and even to find a description of it in a *kaidai*, it is first necessary to know how the title is pronounced. In the vast majority of cases this is no special problem, for most titles consist of ordinary Japanese words (or proper nouns) pronounced in exactly the same way as they would be in any other context. Comparatively few Japanese book titles have irregular or unpredictable pronunciations. For these one must use one's ingenuity, though some guides do exist. *Kokusho kaidai* has a character index of titles described, and as we have said, some large character dictionaries include entries for book titles. Remember that the meaning of a title usually determines its pronunciation. For example, the character 經 may be read in a number of ways, but when it appears in the title of a book that appears to be of Buddhist origin, one can assume that it means *sutra*, and hence should be read *kyō*. It follows that semantic considerations should normally govern one's practice in dividing the words of a title.

Titles of modern books are rarely troublesome. If there is doubt the word of the author may be taken as the final authority on how the title is to be pronounced, though of course he may be unavailable for comment. Publishers of books with irregularly pronounced titles sometimes thoughtfully indicate the

---

[12] See pages 8–9. *Nihon keizai-shi bunken* (Tokyo, 1933).

Nihon keizai-shi shin-bunken (Tokyo, 1942) continues the former to 1941.

Nihon keizai-shi dai-san bunken (Tokyo, 1953) covers 1941–1950.

Keizai-shi nenkan (3 vols.; 1955–56) covers 1951–55.

Keizai-shi bunken is an annual serial which continues the foregoing to date.

[13] *Rekishi-gaku no seika to kadai* (Tokyo, Iwanami Shoten, 1950–58, vols. 1–9). Vols. 7–9 were issued as separate numbers of the journal *Rekishi-gaku kenkyū* (no. 196, June, 1956; no. 213, July, 1957; no. 221, July, 1958).

correct readings with kana placed beside the characters on the title page (*furigana*). If no such indication is given, guess intelligently, using dictionaries where necessary; then, if possible, check your guesses by reference to an alphabetically indexed bibliography. A romanized list (such as a formal bibliography in a Western scholarly work or perhaps the card catalog of a scholarly library) would provide a complete check. So would a list in kana order, all of whose entries were supplied with *furigana*. Any large index of book titles arranged in the order of the Roman or Japanese alphabet may be used as a partial check on the accuracy of one's own romanized transcription, for it will verify the pronunciation of the first word or words of the title. In a few cases, alas, this is the best that one can do.

Some works are known by two or more different titles. Many Buddhist works, for example, bear long titles difficult to remember and are known more commonly by abbreviated names. *Bussho kaisetsu dai jiten* indexes the most common alternative titles, as does the Heibon-sha *Dai jiten*. It is easy enough for the student well versed in Japanese historical literature to make the mental transfer from *Nihon shoki*, as Japanese usually say it, to *Nihongi*, as the book is more likely to be referred to in Western language contexts. Both are wholly acceptable titles for the work, and no possible confusion could result from using either of them. More obscure books are more troublesome. If one did not know that *Gyokuyō* and *Gyokkai* were alternative titles for the same Heian period diary, one could find out by consulting the entry under either name in a *kaidai*, a general literary or historical encyclopedia, or a large linguistic dictionary such as the *Dai jiten* or *Dai Kan-Wa jiten*.

It is always wise for students to consider carefully the meanings of titles, together with the exact implications an author intended in choosing one title instead of another, for the name of a book may disclose information about the author's purpose in writing it.

PROBLEMS OF AUTHORSHIP. In a great many cases the authors of premodern Japanese books are unknown. Even with as well known a book as the *Tale of Genji*, universally ascribed to Murasaki Shikibu, there is some doubt among scholars as to whether that lady had anything to do with the last third of the novel. The *Nihon shoki* is often said to have been written by Prince Toneri, who however was probably no more than an editor of contributions from others. No one has any idea who wrote the *Taiheiki*, and it is thought that the work in its present form is the product of many hands. Japanese *kaidai* devote much space to points such as these. Where the author of a work is known, the *kaidai* usually provide some information about him—who he was, when he lived, and what circumstances prompted him to write the book in question. These reference books, then, function as important biographical sources on authors of books (including, it should be noted, authors who are better known to history for some other activity, such as politics, warfare, or religion).

These are fewer problems of authorship with modern books. Students should take care not to misconstrue the words *hensan-sha* and *henshū-sha*. Both mean "editor," but the man so called on the title page or colophon page of a large reference book or similar publication may not be the one who did the real work of putting it into shape. Sometimes the president of a publishing company assumes the title of editor of many of the joint productions done by his firm. Furthermore, some scholarly books listed as having a certain "author" (*chosha* or *chosaku-sha*) would be more properly described in English as having been *edited* by the man in question. The practice is extremely widespread in the Japanese academic world for a senior teacher or scholar to incorporate the writings of his students or disciples in books published under his own name.

These practices pose a problem for bibliographers, who prefer to confine the information in their citations to what can actually be found inside the book but who would nevertheless like the citations to be accurate. Scholarly practice varies accordingly, as the following pair of acceptable alternatives indicates.

> Shimonaka Yasaburō, ed., *Dai jiten* (26 vols.; Tokyo, Heibon-sha, 1934–36).
>
> *or*
>
> Heibon-sha, comp., *Dai jiten* (26 vols.; Tokyo, published by the compiler, 1934–36).

If a man is credited with authorship of a book, the safest procedure is to cite him as author unless there is positive evidence that others wrote the book in his name. Whatever one's practice one should be aware that the categories by which one refers to the men responsible for modern Japanese publications do not always correspond exactly to those used in the West.

Complete bibliographies of the works of a single author—the really exhaustive kind that list all works, even those that are unimportant or lost—are hard to find for more than a few of the most famous and standard writers. The following are plausible places to look for complete lists and for the next best thing, lists of authors' principal works:

(1) Biographical works, including general and specialized biographical dictionaries.
(2) Author indexes to the *kaidai* and related works discussed in this chapter.
(3) The reasonably inclusive catalogs of very large libraries of Japanese materials, particularly the National Diet Library.
(4) The *Bunka jimmei-roku*, one of whose functions is to register Japanese copyrights.

(5) *Kindai bungaku kenkyū sōsho*, which has been published since 1956 and includes virtually complete lists of works by and works about the major modern men of letters.

DATE OF WRITING. Sometimes the only clue as to when a book was written is a *terminus ante quem* provided by a dated manuscript or reference. In other cases the author's birth and death dates afford the only information that can be known. In others internal evidence is helpful, and in still others there is literally no way of ascertaining within centuries the date of writing. In such matters as these, the *kaidai* and other sources of information mentioned above are necessary reference tools for the modern student, for in them the findings of generations of scholars are summarized and appraised. They also indicate the dates covered by histories, diaries, and other works for which such information is pertinent.

There is usually no explicit statement within a book of modern date as to when it was written. Of course, a date of first publication, if that can be ascertained, may be taken as a rough guide. If the colophon tells you nothing about this, you may find such information in certain of the published catalogs of library holdings referred to in Chapter 1. Going through back issues of publishers' yearbooks until you find the date of original publication of a certain item is another method that sometimes works, but it requires considerable patience.

SIZE OF WORKS. The size of modern publications is almost always indicated in bibliographies and catalogs in numbers of pages or of bound volumes. For premodern works, bibliographers use a unit called *kan* 卷, which corresponds roughly to a chapter. The *kan* of any single work are usually of comparable length, but that is not to say that the unit has unvarying significance for measuring all premodern Japanese books. It is a very rough unit of measure, and should be used accordingly. One can be sure that a work of one *kan* is quite short, say the length of a letter or brief essay, while a work in fifty or more *kan* is quite long, running to two or more volumes in Western-style binding.

The same word, *kan*, is sometimes used with ordinal numerals to specify the numbered bound volumes of a set or the "volumes" of periodicals, which customarily include all issues for separate calendar years. However, the total number of volumes in a set is rarely described in *kan*, but almost always in *satsu*, the more common word for a bound volume.

TEXTUAL AND PUBLISHING HISTORY. Modern scholars of the literary and historical works of older Japan have devoted a great deal of attention to textual problems. Extant manuscript texts of a work, the dates at which they were copied, variations among them, and the history of printed versions of the work are all matters that relate directly to the work's authenticity and its usefulness as a source on the period in which it was originally written. *Kaidai* and encyclopedias do not as a rule include much information on these points, but the introductions to modern scholarly editions of old books usually discuss them in considerable detail. This is one special value to be found in the prefaces to individual works in the great collection of standard historical books, *Kokushi taikei*.[14] The prefaces in *Nihon koten bungaku taikei* discuss textual problems concerning the most famous works of classical literature. Kurita's *Sōgō kokushi kenkyū* is another good reference source on a great number of premodern works of all kinds. Finally, a word should be said about the voluminous writings on manuscripts and printing by Japanese specialists in the field of bibliography. Kawase Kazuma, to name but one example, has written shelves of books, including the gigantic *Nihon shoshi-gaku no kenkyū* (published in 1943), in which the historian may find the solutions to countless of his technical problems concerning texts.

---

[14] Rev. and enlarged; Kuroita Katsumi, ed. (57 vols.; Tokyo, from 1935).

KINDS AND CHARACTER OF WORKS. The description of each work mentioned in a *kaidai* or other reference work contains some indication of what class of work it is: fiction, history, poetry, religious doctrine, or scholarly exegesis, etc. In recognition of the quantity of written sources and the brevity of life, the editors of *kaidai* usually furnish brief summaries of contents as well.

The terminology with which traditional Japanese bibliographers describe classes of historical works is discussed in the following chapter.

BOOK REVIEWS AND CRITICISM. It is often useful in reaching one's own appraisal of a Japanese book to know what other critics have had to say about it. There is unfortunately no reference source that serves the same purpose in locating reviews of current Japanese books as efficiently as the *Book Review Digest* and other similar publications do for those of the West. The closest equivalent (for dates since 1949) is *Zasshi kiji sakuin*, which indexes reviews both by subject and by author of the book reviewed. A special subhead, *shohyō*, under each topic of the index differentiates reviews from other items.

The most likely place to look for critical reviews of scholarly publications would be one or another of Japan's many learned journals that cover almost all academic fields. A haphazard but occasionally fruitful way of finding a review is to find in a list of learned journals[15] those which relate to the field or fields treated in the book in question and go to the issues that were published within a year or two after the first publication of the book. Some learned journals have cumulative indexes —usually by subjects—covering many years of their run. For example, the indexes to the historical journals *Shigaku zasshi*[16]

---

[15] See above, p. 12.

[16] Tōkyō Daigaku Shigakkai, ed. *Shigaku zasshi sō-mokuroku* (Tokyo, 1952). Indexes vols. 1–60, 1889–1951.

and *Shirin*[17] cite book reviews that have appeared in those periodicals from the time of their first publication until after World War II.

THE LOCATION OF BOOKS. The problem of locating a copy of a Japanese work calls for varying methods of solution according to whether the work is (1) an ordinary modern book, filling a whole volume or set of volumes by itself, and with no particular complexities of pubishing history; (2) a work whose copyright is in the public domain, and which is too short for separate publication, or a work which for some other reason is likely to have been printed in larger modern anthologies or collections; or (3) a work which exists only in manuscript or in rare printed edition. The card catalog of the library which you use (or the published catalog of some other library) is an obvious place to go to find out whether the library contains material of the first type, but for materials of the second and third kinds, it is usually necessary to make use of special reference tools.

Standard works, those of the public domain, and those too short to be published by themselves are most likely to be found in the collections of works that are variously called *sōsho*—anthologies; *zenshū*—complete works; or *senshū*—selected works. Some library catalogs contain cards for the individual titles in such collections, but these *analytic cards*, as they are called, are rarely if ever complete for all of the library's holdings. It is therefore necessary to refer to a published index of Japanese *sōsho*. So far the *Nihon sōsho sakuin*,[18] in its revised and enlarged edition, has no real competitors, for it is much larger and more recent than other indexes. Following the title of each work in the index there is a list of the collections in which the work

---

[17] Kyōto Daigaku Shigaku Kenkyū-kai, ed., *Shirin sō-mokuroku* (Kyoto, 1958). Indexes vols. 1–40, 1916–57. Supersedes *Shirin sōmoku sakuin* (Kyoto, 1935), which indexes vols. 1–20, 1916–35.

[18] Hirose Bin, comp. [*Zōtei*] *Nihon sōsho sakuin* (Tokyo, 1957).

may be found. Volume numbers are not specified. This is unfortunate, because some of the collections are very large and are not themselves indexed. A separate section of the *Nihon sōsho sakuin* lists and describes briefly the collections which have been analyzed in the index.

Most of the *kaidai* cite editions or locations in *sōsho* of the books described in them, but in general they are not so complete or so up to date as the *Nihon sōsho sakuin*.

Guides to collections of rare books and manuscripts are mostly cursory in description and incomplete in coverage. The researcher who happens to be in Japan should consult *Chōsa kikan tosho-kan sōran*, the best published guide to the special libraries there, to acquaint himself with the best places to go for certain *kinds* of archival and rare materials. Some special libraries have published more detailed descriptions of their own holdings.[19] That of the Historiographic Materials Compilation Bureau, Tokyo University,[20] is to be specially commended to students of Japanese history.

[19] For a list see *Nihon no sankō tosho*, pp. 15–16.
[20] [*Tōkyō Daigaku*] *Shiryō Hensan-jo tosho mokuroku.*

8. Historical Sources

IN THIS CHAPTER we discuss Japanese histories as well as the main printed collections of source materials for the study of Japanese history. The related and vital matter of unpublished archival materials is too complex for summary treatment here. Large quantities of Japanese historical sources have been printed and more are published each year, so that the student of almost any subject would do best to start with these, leaving the unpublished sources until he has the advice of specialized Japanese archivists or bibliographers.

JAPANESE HISTORIES—THE MAIN TRADITION. Secondary histories in Japan form a continuous tradition dating from the early eighth century. The earliest of them were the *Kojiki* of 712 and the *Nihon shoki* of 720. Certain works finished as recently as the Meiji period, such as the *Zoku Tokugawa jikki* and the *Dai Nihon shi*, were specimens of the same tradition.

The tradition owes its most important features to Chinese practice.[1] The characteristic purposes for which Chinese histories were written—the instruction of rulers and the moral edification of readers—motivated Japanese historians as well and helped shape the contents of their work. Historical forms also followed Chinese precedents closely. In China, the writing of history was "vitally affected by largely formal distinctions

---

[1] The following brief guides are recommended: Charles S. Gardner, *Chinese Traditional Historiography* (Cambridge, Mass., 1938); Han Yu-shan, *Elements of Chinese Historiography* (Hollywood, Calif., 1955).

[between types] which have been canonized by custom."[2]
The same holds for Japan as well, even if one allows for the
qualifications that certain of the important Chinese categories
were not popular in Japan and that the Japanese sometimes
failed to apply the rules that applied to various categories as
rigidly as did their Chinese counterparts.

   In both countries the majority of histories could be classified
into three large groups according to their fundamental principles of organization. The three classes are: (1) those in which
events are dated and arranged in strict chronological order
—*nembetsu* 年別; (2) those consisting of one or more biographies
—*jimbetsu* 人別 ; and (3) those in which each of several whole
trains of events is narrated from beginning to end—*jibetsu* 事別.
The first-named class requires some comment. It is a distinctly
Far Eastern contribution to historiography. Furthermore it
accounts for most of the works that the Japanese themselves
have canonized as especially authoritative or official. A full
history organized by the chronological (*nembetsu*) principle is
known as a *hennen-shi* 編年史—or annals. Such a work
consists of dates arranged chronologically, each date being
followed by a narration of the noteworthy events of that day.
If the reader of a *hennen-shi* wishes to find in it an account
of a complex train of events that extended over many months
or years (a war, say, or the conception, execution, and results
of a fiscal reform) he must piece it together from a text in
which it is most likely to be interwoven with numerous irrelevant matters. If the exact date of an event was unknown
it was fixed into the narrative as accurately as possible at the
end of the section for the appropriate month or year. The form
permitted some slight relaxation of the rules when it was
desirable to indicate in brief some background event which
might explain the dated event under discussion. Otherwise,

---

² Gardner, p. 86.

it was as rigid in its adherence to strict chronology as a diary, a journal, or a chronological table.

The *seishi* 正史 (Chinese, *cheng-shih*)—or standard history— was another of the Chinese categories of histories which had some influence on Japanese historians. This was a hybrid form, consisting of a section of "annals," in which the main events were described, and other sections biographical or topical. This form had been used for the official "dynastic histories" in China and it produced two noteworthy histories in the Tokugawa period, the *Dai Nihon shi* and the *Dai Nihon yashi*.

Whatever the type, the most formal histories of the Sino-Japanese tradition were largely composed of verbatim, or nearly verbatim, extracts from earlier works, and they sometimes incorporated directly the full texts of the relevant primary documents. This means that modern students may find these works of the same usefulness as collections of primary sources. In fact, the earliest known text of some important primary document might well be that found in some secondary history compiled years or centuries later.

Unfortunately, historians did not always identify the sources of their information, even when they quoted them directly. A transcription of an official document might be made directly from the archive in which it was preserved, but on the other hand it might be copied from an earlier secondary work. Spurious documents might in the process become regarded as authentic, and—a more usual danger—successive recopyings might produce deviations from the original text. Where historians pieced a narrative together from a variety of primary and secondary materials, it is not often possible to detect what sources were used. The *Dai Nihon shi* and *Dai Nihon yashi* are exceptions among premodern works, for their authors cited all of their sources in double-column notes.

These are some of the aspects of the Chinese tradition which

Japanese historians made their own. Some other features are important in explaining the qualities of the Japanese historians' craft.

(1) Officially commissioned histories did not play as important a role in Japan as they did in China. The Japanese court produced a number of official histories in the eighth and ninth centuries, but these are far from being as complex or sophisticated as their Chinese counterparts, the *cheng-shih*. Instead, they are straightforward annalistic accounts eked out, in the earliest examples, by myths preserved in a native oral tradition. After the ninth century histories were private and unofficial. Historians might be figures of political prominence, but their works lacked the stamp of imperial authority. In some cases (e.g., the *Ō-kagami*) the loss in authenticity was offset by a gain in human interest, inasmuch as private historians were free to indulge in subjective statements that are often very revealing of themselves and their times, and they were also relieved of an exclusive and confining concern for matters consequential to the state.

(2) Nevertheless, it must be admitted that most histories, even those written by private persons, clung doggedly to political and military themes. With the later histories of a kind especially influenced by Chinese models one should qualify this statement and say that the preponderance of attention was given to affairs of the imperial court, even for periods when the court was ineffectual and effective political power had moved to other agencies. In Japan after the end of the Heian period all of the offices of the imperial system were sinecures, and most of the people who held them were men of no particular historical importance. Nevertheless, in imitation of Chinese practices the histories of Japan that pretended to be national histories (as opposed to accounts of isolated events, or of local or private affairs) continued to record with their dates the vital affairs of these figureheads,

often at the expense of matters of more obvious concern to history.

(3) Concern for accurate dating characterized Japanese as well as Chinese historiography, and for the most part the Japanese were conscientious about finding dates that were historically verifiable. In some cases, however, the concern that events be dated degenerated into an attempt to assign dates even where none could possibly be known. For example, the authors of the *Nihon shoki* falsified much of the protohistorical material which had come down to them by arbitrarily assigning years, months, and dates to each event.

(4) Taboos against frank discussion of the ruler or his ancestors sometimes inhibited historical objectivity in China. However, the many changes of dynasty meant that eventually a state of affairs would come about in which it would be possible to discuss governmental matters of the past objectively. In Japan, the fact that there had never been a change of imperial dynasty prevented until recently the frank appraisal of imperial rule, even that of very early times. Where non-imperial rulers (e.g., shoguns) were concerned, the taboos did not apply beyond the fall from power of the ruler's family.

There follows a brief check list of some of the most important works in the main tradition of Japanese historiography. Citations include the significant translations of all or parts of these works into Western languages.

1. *Kojiki* 古事記. Completed 712. Coverage to 592. Trans. by Basil Hall Chamberlain, *Translation of "Ko-ji-ki" or "Records of Ancient Matters"* (Kobe, 1932). The oldest extant Japanese history. Frequently called the first extended work intended to represent the Japanese language with Chinese characters, though much of it seems to have been intended as pure Chinese. Commissioned by imperial

order. Incorporates much legendary and protohistorical material.

The Six National Histories (*Rikkoku-shi* 六國史):

2. *Nihon shoki* 日本書紀. Completed 720. Coverage to 697. (Also called *Nihongi* 日本紀). Trans. by W. G. Aston, *Nihongi; Chronicles of Japan from the Earliest Times to 697* (London, 1956).

3. *Shoku Nihongi* 續日本紀. Coverage 697–791. Trans. by J. B. Snellen, "Shoku Nihongi; Chronicles of Japan, Continued A.D. 697–791 (Books I–VI)," *Transactions of the Asiatic Society of Japan*, 2nd. ser., 11 (1934), pp. 151–239; 14 (1937), pp. 209–278.

4. *Nihon kōki* 日本後紀. Coverage 792–833. Extant portions cover 796–816.

5. *Shoku Nihon kōki* 續日本後紀. Coverage 833–850.

6. *Nihon Montoku Tennō jitsuroku* 日本文德天皇實錄. Coverage 850–858.

7. *Nihon sandai jitsuroku* 日本三代實錄. Coverage 858–887. Six works in Chinese compiled under imperial auspices and forming a continuous account of Japanese history from mythological times to 887. The first includes legendary material similar to that in the *Kojiki*, though the two works frequently supplement, and sometimes contradict, each other. The later portions of the *Nihon shoki* and all of the other five histories are annalistic in form and imperial-centered in scope. In these respects they are the pattern-setters for most of the Chinese-language works listed below.

8. *Sendai kuji hongi* 先代舊事本紀. Completed about 901–922. Coverage to 620. Largely a duplication of early portions of *Nihon shoki*, but including some additional material presumably based on sources no longer extant.

9. *Kogo shūi* 古語拾遺. By Imbe no Hironari. Completed

807. Coverage to about 700. Written to demonstrate the past glories of the Imbe family and its connections with the Nakatomi (Fujiwara).

10. *Ruijū kokushi* 類聚國史. Attributed to Sugawara Michizane. Completed 892. Arranged topically under categories such as Shinto, the imperial house, Buddhism, and manners and customs.

11. *Nihon kiryaku* 日本紀略. Coverage to 1036.
Numbers 8-11 are important sources for early Japanese history supplementary to the Six National Histories.

12. *Shin kokushi* 新國史. By Fujiwara Saneyori. Completed 950–954. No longer extant. The last of the official histories.

13. *Geki nikki* 外記日記. No longer extant. An official daily chronicle of early Heian times.

14. *Honchō seiki* 本朝世紀. Extant sections cover 935–1154. Thought to preserve portions of numbers 12 and 13, above. Contains some unique information.

15. *Fusō ryakki* 扶桑略記. Written 12th century (?). Coverage to 1094. Part lost. A brief informal history of Japan by a twelfth-century priest Ajari Kōen. It includes quotations from some important primary sources otherwise lost.

16. *Hyaku renshō* 百錬抄. Written late Kamakura period.

17. *Zokushi gushō* 續史愚抄. Coverage 1260–1780. Continuation of the above.

18. *Teiō hennen-ki* 帝王編年記. Coverage to 1301.

19. *Ichidai yōki* 一代要記. Coverage to 1318.

20. *Rekidai kōki* 歴代皇記. Coverage to 1477.

21. *Kōnendai ryakki* 皇年代略記. Coverage to 1611.

22. *Kōdai-ki* 皇代記. Coverage to 1380.
Annalistic works in Chinese. They perpetuated the aristocratic or court tradition of historiography that had begun with the Six National Histories, but in an age in which

the center of the nation's life had passed from the court
to provincial or military families.

23. *Mizu kagami* 水鏡. Completed about the end of the Heian
    period. Coverage to 850.
24. *Ō-kagami* 大鏡. Probably written early 12th century.
    Coverage 850–1025. Trans. by Joseph K. Yamagiwa,
    "The *Ōkagami*; The Sections on Michinaga and the
    Stories of the Fujiwara Clan," *Translations from Early
    Japanese Literature* (Cambridge, Mass., 1951), pp. 271–374.
25. *Ima kagami* 今鏡. Completed 1170. Coverage 1026–1170.
26. *Masu kagami* 増鏡. Completed about 1374. Coverage 1185–
    1333.
    Works in Japanese less formal than the preceding. They
    treat political history and the private affairs of individuals
    at the court. The *Ō-kagami*, which was the pattern
    setter, deals primarily with the fortunes of the Fujiwara
    family at the height of their power. Curiously, numbers 23,
    24, and 26 are the works customarily specified as members
    of this genre and labeled the "three *kagami*" (*san-kagami*).

27. *Eiga monogatari* 榮華物語. Coverage *c.* 888–1092. Similar
    in style to the *kagami*. Concerned principally with the
    glories of the Fujiwara family. May have been written by
    an eye-witness of some of the later events described.

28. *Heike monogatari* 平家物語. Trans. by A. L. Sadler, "The
    Heike Monogatari," *Transactions of the Asiatic Society of
    Japan*, 46, 2 (1918), pp. 1–278; 49, 1 (1921), pp. 1–354.
29. *Gempei seisui-ki* 源平盛衰記.
30. *Hōgen monogatari* 保元物語.
31. *Heiji monogatari* 平治物語. Trans. by Edwin O. Reischauer,
    "The *Heiji Monogatari*," *Translations from Early Japanese
    Literature*, pp. 377–457.
    Four important works of late Heian or early Kamakura
    date (at least in their original forms). The authorship of

each is unknown or disputed and the textual history is exceedingly complex. All of them deal with the greatness of the Taira family and its struggles with the rival Minamoto. Though not the first works of the genre of semi-historical writing known as *gunki monogatari* (battle tales), they are the first great examples and the models for later works of the kind.

32. *Azuma kagami* 吾妻鏡. Coverage 1180–1266. Written between 1268 and 1301. Minoru Shinoda, *The Founding of the Kamakura Shogunate, 1180–1185; With Selected Translations from the Azuma Kagami* (New York, 1960). The most important work dealing with the history of the early years of the Kamakura Shogunate.

33. *Taiheiki* 太平記. Written 14th century. Coverage 1318–67. Trans. by Helen Craig McCullough, *The Taiheiki; A Chronicle of Medieval Japan* (New York, 1959). The last of the great *gunki monogatari*, and like numbers 28–31, not a fully historical work. Deals with the fall of the Kamakura Shogunate, the Restoration of the Emperor Go-Daigo, and the early years of the Ashikaga Shogunate.

34. *Gukanshō* 愚管抄. By Jien (or Jichin). Completed 1220. Trans. by J. Rahder, "Miscellany of Personal Views of an Ignorant Fool," *Acta Orientalia*, 15 (1936), pp. 173–230. Called the first interpretative history in Japanese from the fact that Jien appended to it an essay on Japanese polity. The body of the work is an annalistic account from the foundation of the imperial line to Jien's own time.

35. *Jinnō shōtō-ki* 神皇正統記. By Kitabatake Chikafusa. Written *c.* 1339. Trans. by Hermann Bohner, *Jinnō-shōtō-ki; Buch von der wahren Gottkaiser-herrschafts-linie* (Tokyo, 1935). The preface gives Chikafusa's ideas on legitimacy, in support of the Southern (Yoshino) line in the period of dynastic schism that followed the fall of the Kamakura

Shogunate. The body of the work is annalistic and covers Japanese history to Chikafusa's time.

36. *Baishōron* 梅松論. Probably written about 1349.

37. *Hōryaku kanki* 保暦間記. Coverage 1156–1339.
Numbers 36 and 37 are of lesser importance for Kamakura and early Ashikaga history. The former is particularly good on the career of Ashikaga Takauji.

38. *Kaei sandai-ki* 花營三代記. Coverage 1367–1425. A political history of the Ashikaga Shogunate in the reigns of the third, fourth, and fifth shoguns.

39. *Nobunaga-ki* (*Shinchō-ki*) 信長記. By Ose Hoan. Completed 1604.

40. *Nobunaga kō-ki* (*Shinchō kō-ki*) 信長公記. By Ōda Gyūichi. Written about 1600.

41. *Hoan Taikō-ki* 甫庵大閤記. By Ose Hoan. Dated 1617.
Three among many informal histories dealing with the period of reunification (late sixteenth century).

42. *Honchō tsugan* 本朝通鑑. Compiled under the direction of Hayashi Razan, *et al.* Covers to 1611. Written 1644–1670. The compilers were of the official academy of the Tokugawa Shogunate and were the chief custodians in Japan of the Orthodox or Ch'eng-Chu School of neo-Confucianism. The work may have been intended as the shogunate's official history of Japan, but it was never so recognized and was unpublished until recent times.

43. *Kokushi jitsuroku* 國史實錄. Compiled by Hayashi Shunsai. Based on the preceding.

44. *Dai Nihon shi* 大日本史. Written 1656–1906. Coverage to 1392. In the form of the Chinese *cheng-shih*. Compiled by neo-Confucian scholars of the court of the daimyos of Mito. An early exponent of the *kinnō*, or imperial loyalist, tradition.

45. *Dai Nihon yashi* 大日本野史. By Iida Tadahiko. Completed

1852. Coverage 1392–1841. Intended as a continuation of the preceding, which it resembles in organization and emphasis.

46. *Chūchō jijitsu* 中朝事實. By Yamaga Sokō.
47. *Tokushi yoron* 讀史餘論. By Arai Hakuseki.
48. *Koshi-tsū* 古史通. By Arai Hakuseki.
49. *Nihon seiki* 日本政記. By Rai San'yō.
50. *Nihon gaishi* 日本外史. By Rai San'yō.
    The authors of numbers 46–50 were all leading scholars of the Tokugawa period, and their works are representative of their respective points of view toward polity, legitimacy, or historiography.

51. *Nochi kagami* 後鑑. By Narushima Ryōjō. Written before 1853. Coverage 1331–1605. Commissioned by the Tokugawa Shogunate. Largely a history of the Ashikaga Shogunate.
52. *Tokugawa jikki* 德川實紀. Compiled by Narushima Motonao. Completed 1849. Officially commissioned by the Tokugawa government as the history of the Tokugawa Shogunate (to 1786).
53. *Zoku Tokugawa jikki* 續德川實紀. The continuation of the preceding, compiled from shogunal archives after the Meiji Restoration.

THE *Dai Nihon Shiryō* AND OTHER COLLECTIONS OF SOURCES. Since early Meiji the Japanese government has given the greatest encouragement to the collection and publication of sources for earlier Japanese history, and two of its agencies, the Shiryō Hensan-jo (Historiographical Institute) and the Ishin Shiryō Hensan-kai (later called Ishin Shiryō Hensan Jimu-kyoku—Office for the Compilation of Materials on the History of the Restoration) have produced the most important collections. The former organization is now affiliated with Tokyo University, and since World War II it has also taken over the work of the latter.

The historiographic work of the modern Japanese government dates from an Imperial Ordinance of 1869, directing that materials be collected for the compilation of an official history of Japan. The history was to be in Chinese. In other respects as well it was to follow the pattern established by the Six National Histories, and it was to cover the period from 887, when the last of the Six Histories breaks off. The work as such never materialized, but the sources which were collected as the basis for it became the nucleus of the compilation known as the *Dai Nihon shiryō*.[3]

The editors of this work have placed all sources in chronological order under heads representing noteworthy historic events. For each head they have written a brief description of the event in modern literary Japanese, and if one were to read all of the descriptions completed or planned from first to last one would have a detailed annalistic history (*hennen-shi*) of Japan from 887 to 1680. Following each descriptive head there appear the texts of all supporting documents. The majority of these are primary sources on the matters in question, but in numerous instances the editors have also included secondary sources, interpretative essays, or even fictional accounts, if these offered information for which no earlier substantiation could be found. The editors have sometimes appended notes discussing discrepancies between different sources on the same event or on other points of historicity.

The work poses problems for users because it is so large, but its contents are arranged logically and even a brief familiarity with the principles involved in its arrangement will greatly facilitate its use. The entire set is divided into twelve sections dealing with periods of from fifteen to two hundred years.

---

[3] Tōkyō Daigaku Shiryō Hensan-jo, comp. (Tokyo, from 1901).

The volume numbers start over again with each section. The publication of each section has been proceeding independently and simultaneously. So far (1962) only one of the sections is complete, and there are therefore gaps at the ends of sections. Here is a list of all the sections and the years covered in the volumes that have been published to date:

SECTION	COMPLETED TO VOLUME	DATE
1. (887–986)	11	967
2. (986–1086)	13	1018
3. (1086–1185)	18	1117
4. (1185–1221)	15	1221
5. (1221–1333)	21	1247
6. (1333–97)	33	1371
7. (1397–1466)	18	1414
8. (1467–1508)	25	1489
9. (1508–68)	13	1522
10. (1568–82)	11	1573
11. (1582–1603)	12	1585
12. (1603–80)	43	1622

A thirteenth section, to cover the period from 1680 to 1867, has been contemplated but publication of it has not been started.

In order to locate sources on a certain event in the *Dai Nihon shiryō* it is desirable to know the date of the event as exactly as possible. The problem is therefore best approached by means of a reasonably complete *nempyō*, or set of chronological tables, for Japanese history. The two best *nempyō* for the purpose, because they are the largest, are *Kokushi dai nempyō* and *Bunka dai nempyō*.

With the date of the event in mind one goes directly to the *Dai Nihon shiryō*, each volume of which indicates on the spine the inclusive dates of coverage. Within each volume there is a detailed table of contents giving the editor's descriptive heads for each event in abbreviated form, and titles of the sources included or of the larger works from which they have been extracted.

Much the same information as appears in the table of contents may be found in the *Shiryō sōran*,[4] a companion publication of the Shiryō Hensan-jo. Each volume of the *Sōran* corresponds to a large block of volumes of the *Shiryō*. Publication of the former is always ahead of that of corresponding sections of the latter, and the *Sōran* may therefore be used as a guide to sources which have not yet appeared in print.

The *Dai Nihon shiryō* unfortunately fails to identify the sources it includes except by titles of whole works, and there is as yet no published index or catalog of materials used. Readers are advised to consult the materials described in the preceding chapter for information on authorship, date of writing, and the general character of sources, for such information may have a vital bearing on the historicity of the accounts.

Where the editors could not date events exactly they did so approximately, placing the sources for these events after the more precisely datable material for the month or year. Materials of biographical interest which relate to a man's whole life or to his character rather than to any datable event in his career appear with the date of his death.

The variety of source materials in the work is vast, including formal histories, government documents, letters, journals, biographies, temple records, and family archives, to name only a few. The volumes on sixteenth- and seventeenth-century history even include many documents in Western languages, in recognition of the importance which the eyewitness accounts of European visitors to Japan have for the study of that period.

The editorial principles adopted for the *Dai Nihon shiryō* apply as well to most of the other collections mentioned below. All

---

[4] Tōkyō Daigaku Shiryō Hensan-jo, comp. (Tokyo, from 1925).

sources appear in the original languages and styles, the only contribution of the editors being to transcribe script forms into movable type. Editors' notes supply probable readings of illegibilities or mistakes in the originals.

Materials on the economic and social history of the Tokugawa period are so voluminous that they justified the Shiryō Hensan-jo's creating an additional series for them. This is the *Dai Nihon kinsei-shiryō*, begun in 1953 and still in the early stages of its publication, which when finished will contain many independent subseries, each comprising some whole large archival collection of a family, a temple, or a local or *han* government.

The Shiryō Hensan-jo has also been compiling a third series, the *Dai Nihon ko-monjo* (since 1901), each of whose three subseries contains materials which do not fit easily into the other two collections. One, subtitled *Hennen monjo*, includes documents of the eighth century, arranged chronologically. A second subseries is known as *Iewake monjo* and comprises whole archival collections of families, temples, or shrines during the period covered by the *Dai Nihon shiryō*.

The remaining subseries, subtitled *Bakumatsu gaikoku kankei monjo*, deals with foreign relations in the Bakumatsu period. The inclusive dates when finished will be 1853 to 1868. The format is similar to that of the *Dai Nihon shiryō*.

In 1911, the Ishin Shiryō Hensan-kai was established as a bureau of the Ministry of Education concerned with the history of the Meiji Restoration. During the war, it published the *Ishin shi*,[5] a large history of the Restoration of rather old-fashioned historiographical principles and with a historical point of view favorable to the governing oligarchy of Meiji Japan. A contribution of perhaps more lasting importance to scholarship is the still unfinished documentary collection *Dai*

---

[5] Ishin Shiryō Hensan Jimukyoku, comp. (6 vols.; Tokyo, 1941–43).

Nihon Ishin shiryō.[6] In organization it is similar to the *Dai Nihon shiryō*. When finished it will deal with the period from 1846 to 1871.

One other series of collected documents, that of the Nihon Shiseki Kyōkai, deserves specific mention. The series has no title, properly speaking, but it is normally referred to as the Nihon Shiseki Kyōkai *sōsho*.[7] It consists of seventy-two separate subseries, each containing documents relating to some particular individual, locality, or event noteworthy in Bakumatsu or Restoration times.

Other privately published documentary collections tend to be smaller and of more specific relevance, and they raise no special problems. For a list of the more important of them, see John W. Hall, *Japanese History: A Guide to Japanese Reference and Research Materials* (pages 47–64).

CLASSIFIED SOURCES—THE *Koji Ruien* AND ITS USE. In this section we deal with those collections of sources which are classified not by date but by general topic head. There are two principal modern works of this kind, the *Koji ruien* and the *Kōbunko*.[8]

The *Koji ruien* is Japan's best known encyclopedia of the traditional Chinese variety; that is, the topic heads instead of being in alphabetical order are arranged according to similarity of subject matter, and the contents consist of primary or other early sources on each topic introduced by brief essays by the editors.

The *Koji ruien* is the outgrowth of a project undertaken in 1879 by the Ministry of Education at the behest of the educator and scholar Nishimura Shigeki, in an attempt to make available the entire range of information regarding Japan's pre-Restoration tradition. The chief limitations of scope are

[6] Tokyo Daigaku Shiryō Hensan-jo, comp. (Tokyo, 1938–).
[7] Nihon Shiseki Kyōkai, comp. (188 vols.; Tokyo, 1915–31).
[8] Mozume Takami, comp. (20 vols.; Tokyo, 1916).

that all materials relate to Japan before 1868 and that material of purely biographical character seems to have been systematically excluded. At times the materials seem to have been selected for capricious reasons, for some of them tell the reader what he already knows about the subject or what he does not want to know. Nevertheless the work is of great value for its extraordinarily wide coverage and the copiousness of documentation for each topic from sources spanning a great range of date. A complete table of contents and a kana index of topic heads are in the last volume.

The *Kōbunko* is similar in character to *Koji ruien* except that its arrangement is alphabetical (by kana), it concentrates more heavily on literary and cultural subjects than does the other work, and it lacks editorial matter of any kind by the editor. It was compiled by the Meiji period writer Mozume Takami. The same author earlier prepared a guide to reference sources on literary and historical topics which he called *Gunsho sakuin*.[9] This is merely an alphabetical list of subject heads each of which is followed by names of works treating them. The *Kōbunko* contains the same subject heads, but includes full texts of most (not all) of the sources cited in the other work.

ORIENTAL AND WESTERN TRADITIONS. At least three strains of historiographic tradition may be detected in the work of contemporary Japanese historians. One of them is the classic Sino-Japanese tradition already referred to. A second might be called the main tradition of European and American historiography. The third tradition is the Marxian.

Influences of the classic Sino-Japanese tradition tend to be more subtle than they are obvious. Few or no pure specimens of the type have been written since the *Dai Nihon shi* and *Koji ruien*, finished in 1906 and 1914 respectively. Some

---

[9] Mozume Takami, comp. (3 vols.; Tokyo, 1916).

positive and negative traits of modern historians continue to reflect the practices of premodern times. A documentary collection like the *Dai Nihon shiryō* is at the same time a documentary history, similar in its fundamentals to the classic *hennen-shi*, for the documents in it are supplemented with dates, abbreviated descriptions, and textual notes supplied by the editors. Perhaps the relatively great importance which Japanese give to chronological tables (*nempyō*) as historical reference works is traceable to the fact that the *hennen-shi*, from the Confucian *Spring and Autumn Annals* downward, was itself a kind of chronological table with the data written out in full sentences rather than being represented graphically. Premodern tradition may also account for the slowness with which modern Japanese scholars have taken to Western habits of source citation. Many modern works of history, including quite excellent ones, cite no sources at all. Others indicate the sources used only by means of a single bibliography at the end. Still others cite sources by titles of works without indicating where in the work the substantiating data may be found.

One example of a more subtle influence of premodern historiographic tradition is to be seen in the customary treatment which prewar Japanese historians in the main gave to the Meiji Restoration. The very name "Restoration" reflects an idea traceable to Confucian thought that the processes of institutional history are basically degenerative, but that from time to time a sudden upsurge of morality may achieve a return of institutions to their pristine condition of ancient times. The view lingered among Japanese historians until World War II that the overthrow of the Tokugawa Shogunate and substitution of a new government under the emperor had been such a renewal of morality.

Another influence of older historical thought was the enshrinement as an unquestionable article of historians' and the public's faith of the mythology which appeared in the *Kojiki* and *Nihon shoki* pertaining to the origins of the Japanese nation. Empiric historians might inwardly disbelieve the myth or discount it as unverifiable, but they ran a real risk of loss of positions, or worse, if they publicly said so.

Despite these survivals from the past, the writing of history from the late nineteenth century on belonged more to the Western than to the Oriental tradition. To indicate the profound changes in historiography which exposure to Western models brought about, one need mention only a few: histories dealing with economic, social, and cultural affairs in addition to the political and military matters that predominated overwhelmingly before; the discovery of new principles of periodization other than ruling families or locations of the capital; more flexible modes of historical narrative than the rigid *hennen-shi* form permitted; and the use of new scholarly disciplines as tools of historical scholarship, such as linguistics, archaeology, psychology, sociology, and modern scientific economics.

The Marxian tradition deserves special attention because of the profound influence it has had on contemporary Japanese scholars. Not all Japanese historians are Marxists by any means, but even those who are not frequently frame their arguments in the context of the Marxian dialectic and make use of Marxian vocabulary.

Marxian historiography begins with the assumption that human history has a single inevitable goal, a Communist society, toward which it proceeds through a limited number of precisely definable stages with well-marked junctures between them. The agents of history are social classes defined by reference to their relations to means of production. The motive power for historical change is the irreconcilable conflicts between social classes. The stages of history, the transitions from one to another, and the classes themselves have been defined and labeled by Marxists, and the labels comprise a distinctive vocabulary that pervades the work of Marxian historians. If one reads their works one should be armed with a specialized dictionary of terms, such as *Kyōsan-shugi jiten*.[10] The book is helpful, but not perfect, for it too presupposes a certain basic familiarity with Marxian assumptions and issues. For that only wide reading will suffice.

MODERN SECONDARY HISTORIES. John W. Hall's *Japanese History: A Guide to Japanese Reference and Research Materials* includes (pages 81–88) the best guide to general survey histories of Japan and narrative histories of particular periods. The same author, in collaboration with Hugh Borton, published in 1961 a briefer but somewhat more up-to-date guide along similar principles in *The American Historical Association's Guide to Historical Literature* (pages 296–318).

DOCUMENTARY COLLECTIONS, NEWSPAPERS, AND OTHER MODERN SOURCES. We have already discussed collections of premodern sources (up to about 1880). We now treat locations of the corresponding materials of general relevance for modern history, deferring until the following chapter laws and other matters of government record.

Declassified materials drawn from government archives of the Meiji period were published as *Hisho ruisan*.[11] Itō Hirobumi was the titular editor and one may surmise that the documents which were selected were such as to present a generally favorable picture of the governing oligarchy of which he was a leading member. Still, the collection occupies a central position on account of the importance of the matters which it deals with. Subsections within it relate to Sino-Japanese relations; the framing of the Constitution of 1889; foreign

---

[10] Hosokawa Karoku and Kawakami Kan'ichi, comps., *Kyōsan-shugi jiten* "*Pocket Dictionary of Communism*" (Tokyo, 1949).

[11] Hisho Ruisan Kankō-kai, comp. (27 vols.; Tokyo, 1933–36).

relations in general; the legal system; the Imperial Diet; finance; the civil service; and military affairs.

Documents relating to Japanese foreign relations call for special treatment. Although some may be found in practically all of the collections mentioned or alluded to here, the most important sources are the serial publications regularly issued by the Japanese Foreign Ministry. The Ministry is publishing its principal archival materials under the title *Nihon gaikō bunsho*. The initial date is 1868, and publication is now complete for virtually all of the Meiji period. In addition to the main series, the *Nihon gaikō bunsho* contains a separate subseries of six volumes dealing with the revision of Japan's initial unequal treaties with Western countries. Documents of this subseries date from 1871 to 1894.

A separate series, issued from 1922 by the Foreign Ministry, *Gaimu-shō kōhyō-shū*, consists of unclassified materials which are permitted to be published immediately for purposes of public notification.

To provide a partial record in documentary form of the entire sweep of Japanese foreign relations from 1854 to 1954, the Foreign Ministry has also published a two-volume set, *Nihon gaikō nempyō narabi ni shuyō bunsho*.[12] This is a good initial source to consult for the most important materials on foreign relations and it is, so far, the only printed source for many documents dating from the Taishō and Shōwa periods.

Japan's defeat and the confiscation by the occupying powers of many of its governmental archives made publicly available a great volume of materials the publication of which would otherwise have been decades in the future if not entirely unlikely. The confiscated archives of the Foreign, Army, Navy, and other ministries were housed for several years in the Library of Congress, and then in the late 1950s

---

[12] Gaimu-shō, comp. (2 vols.; Tokyo, 1955).

returned to Japan. In the meantime, a large selection of
Foreign Ministry archives had been placed on microfilm,
copies of which exist in several American libraries. A check
list has been published.[13]

Materials in the archives of the other ministries had not
been filmed until 1957, when the decision had already been
made to return them. A group of American scholars then
worked with great haste to place on films those documents that
seemed most important, and they had time to complete about
four-fifths of the work which they had projected. Copies of the
films exist in the Library of Congress and elsewhere, and
there is a printed check list of them.[14] The use of these various
archival materials is further facilitated by a bibliographic
guide by James Morley.[15]

Back files of daily newspapers are obvious repositories of
historical source materials. Reduced type editions on durable
paper (*shukusatsu-ban*) of the principal Tokyo dailies have been
issued for the past several decades. In addition, there are now
available in some American libraries microfilm runs of important papers from the early Meiji period.[16] From time to time
the papers themselves, or other agencies, publish in book
form selected newspaper articles from the past. Few of these
are compendious enough to have much scholarly value, but
there are two signal exceptions. The *Bakumatsu Meiji shimbun*

[13] Cecil H. Uyehara, *Checklist of Archives in the Japanese Ministry of Foreign
Affairs, Tokyo, Japan, 1868–1945* (Washington, 1954).

[14] John Young, *Checklist of Microfilm Reproductions of Selected Archives of the Japanese
Army, Navy, and Other Government Agencies, 1868–1945* (Washington, 1959).

[15] "Check List of Seized Japanese Records in the National Archives," *The Far
Eastern Quarterly*, IX, 3 (May, 1950), pp. 306–33.

On archives associated with the International Military Tribunal (Tokyo
War Crimes Trial), see below, pages 124–25.

[16] The Japan Publications Trading Co., Ltd. has prepared films of the following
runs: Asahi Shimbun, from July, 1888; Mainichi Shimbun, from February, 1872;
Yomiuri Shimbun, from November, 1874; Nihon Keizai Shimbun, from January,
1945.

zenshū[17] is a collection of newspaper articles from the earliest days of modern newspapers in Japan. It covers the period from 1861 to 1870. For the entire Meiji period, there is a large compilation, the *Shimbun shūsei Meiji hennen-shi*,[18] put together from newspapers and a certain number of other serial publications. The excellent index of subjects and people's names makes this a convenient reference source on the major events as well as the minutiae of Meiji history.

The sixteen-volume *Nihon kokusei jiten* would appear from the title to be an encyclopedia of politics, but it is actually a rich collection of sources of general relevance to Japanese history. When finished it will treat the period from 1885 to the present. The materials include official and other primary sources, eked out with newspaper accounts and the like, to provide a full picture of the political, economic, social, and cultural life of Japan in modern times. The arrangement is according to a complex mixture of chronological and topical principles, but the table of contents helps.

[17] Meiji Bunka Kenkyū-kai, comp. (5 vols.; Tokyo, 1934–35).
[18] Nakayama Yasumasa, ed. (15 vols.; Tokyo, 1935–40).

9. Laws and Other Official Sources

THIS CHAPTER is designed for students of Japanese history and society in general and will not meet the more specialized requirements of lawyers and legal scholars. Even non-specialists should be familiar with some basic bibliographic guides. The official bibliographies listing current publications of the Japanese government are discussed in Chapter 1. They are classified by subject, and are useful in determining whether reference material on a given field has been published in a certain year. *Sengo hōgaku bunken sō-mokuroku*[1] lists Japanese language postwar legal materials of all kinds. *An Index to Japanese Law, 1867–1961*[2] lists materials in English. Robert Ward's bibliography of materials on political science in the University of Michigan's bibliographical series affords one of the best existing guides to the use of legal materials. Further information on specific works may be found in *Kokushi bunken kaisetsu*. There is also a useful chapter on "general reference materials" in *Hōgaku kenkyū no shiori*,[3] a students' guide to the bibliography of the study of law by several specialists from the Faculty of Law of Tokyo University.[4]

[1] Hōritsu Jihō Henshū-bu, ed. (2 vols.; Tokyo, 1954–55).

[2] "Preliminary draft of a complete bibliography of all books, pamphlets, articles, essays, statutes, cases, and other legal materials concerning Japanese law in the English language." Conference on Japanese Law, Harvard Law School, September, 1961. (Mimeographed.)

[3] Kikui Tsunahiro, Yokota Kisaburō, and Wagatsuma Sakae, comps. (2 vols.; Tokyo, 1950).

[4] Mr. Cho Sung Yoon of the staff of the Library of Congress is preparing a more comprehensive guide in English to the law and legal literature of Japan.

Kampō, THE OFFICIAL GAZETTE. The first official publication for libraries to get and for students to know is *Kampō*—or
The Official Gazette. This is a daily public record which the
central government has published since 1883 attesting or
describing all of its important acts and proceedings. No other
source is as authoritative, and students are advised to refer to
it and cite it whenever they need an official statement about
some affair of the government.

The contents of *Kampō* are of two kinds: matters of law and
matters of information. In the former category are the official
texts of all statutes passed by the Diet or other competent
authority, ministerial and other administrative edicts, and
treaties. The latter category consists of all kinds of official
announcements: elections of Diet members and governors;
appointments of Cabinet members, Privy Councilors, and
other high civil officials; first commissions and promotions of
military officers; conferral of titles of nobility or of decorations;
appointment of teachers in state-supported schools; official
daily reports of astronomical, seismic, weather, and tide
conditions; palace announcements; and summaries of the
economic conditions of Japan and Japan's overseas possessions.
The prewar *Kampō* even included abstracts of all doctoral
dissertations accepted by the Ministry of Education, which
until after World War II was the sole grantor of that degree.

Each day's issue of *Kampō* carries its own table of contents,
and a cumulative subject index is published every month.
Note that the monthly index is published as a supplement to
some regular daily issue published in the following month.
The exact date of the month on which the index is published
varies, but may be found in the official bibliographies.

An English-language version of *Kampō* was published during
the Occupation, with the title *Official Gazette*.[5]

[5] The exact dates are April 1, 1946, to April 28, 1952.

There is no exact counterpart to *Kampō* for dates prior to 1883. The closest is the *Dajōkan nisshi*, a record of the proceedings of the Dajōkan, or Council of State, from 1868 to 1877. This work exists in an exceedingly rare original edition, and has been reprinted as a major part of the *Ishin nisshi*,[6] which also includes several other documents recording the business of the early Meiji government.

THE DIET. Japan's national legislature is known as *Kokkai*, the National Diet. Under the 1889 Constitution it was called *Teikoku Gikai*, the Imperial Diet. Since 1890, its function has been to legislate the principal national statutes of the country. It has been a bicameral body from the start. Before World War II it consisted of a House of Peers (*Kizoku-in*) and a House of Representatives (*Shūgi-in*). The 1947 Constitution replaced the House of Peers with the wholly elected House of Councilors (*Sangi-in*).

As with other national parliaments in modern times, part of the business of each house of the Diet is conducted by the house as a whole, but far more of it by committees charged with considering specialized kinds of legislation. When a house of the Diet meets as a whole, it records its debates and proceedings in a supplement to *Kampō* known as *Kampō Gōgai*: *Kizoku-in* (or *Sangi-in*, or *Shūgi-in*) *giji sokki-roku*. These are stenographic transcriptions of floor debates; in other words, the equivalent of America's *Congressional Record*. Like *Kampō*, the publication is issued every business day. Debates of committees, which may be of very great importance, are recorded in special publications for each house of the Diet.

Publications so voluminous as the *Giji sokki-roku* are difficult for the casual student to use. If his interest lies in the period before 1928, he may consult an abridgment, the *Dai Nihon*

---

[6] Hashimoto Hiroshi, ed. (20 vols.; Shizuoka, Tokyo, 1932–35).

Teikoku Gikai-shi,[7] which duplicates much of the information in *Giji sokki-roku*, but in more manageable form. This publication also contains summaries of important legislative matters, as well as biographies of Diet members. The best substitute for dates later than 1928 is probably accounts of legislative sessions appearing in the great metropolitan newspapers.

The Japanese Diet publishes an indispensable source on the election of its own members. It is known as *Shūgi-in* (or *Sangi-in*) *sō-senkyo ichiran* and contains statistics on the vote cast for every candidate, broken down by electoral districts. It also records the number of registered voters in each district, broken down by party and sex. In short, it duplicates the information on general elections that can be found in the Japanese newspapers and yearbooks after each election, but it is published officially and hence is more authoritative.

LAWS AND ORDINANCES. Japanese laws are referred to by a variety of terms usually denoting the issuing authority or the way in which they were issued. There are some differences in terminology between prewar and postwar Japan, but in both periods laws may be divided into three main classes; statutes (*hōritsu*) enacted by the Diet, ordinances or orders (*rei*) issued by executive organs; and treaties and other international agreements.

The terminology for executive enactments is complex. In prewar Japan the emperor was the highest executive authority. The Cabinet, Privy Council, and administration actually made most of the decisions of state, but they did so in the emperor's name and consequently described many of their pronouncements as emanating from him. Hence, the ordinary decrees made by the top administrative echelons were known as Imperial Ordinances (*chokurei*). Some of these dealt with

[7] Dai Nihon Teikoku Gikai-shi Kankō-kai, comp. (18 vols.; Tokyo, Shizuoka, 1926–30).

matters outside the constitutional competence of the Diet and are known as Prerogative Ordinances. Others were Extraordinary Ordinances (*kinkyū chokurei*), proclaimed when the Diet was not in session. These remained effective until the Diet met and decided to ratify or reject them. The emperor occasionally issued decrees of broad general application known as Rescripts (*chokugo*), but these were not considered to be part of the regular body of law.

With the 1947 Constitution the emperor lost his ordinance-making power. The Cabinet, however, continues to have some legislative functions. Its decrees are called Cabinet Ordinances (*seirei*). Executive Ordinances issued by the military services before World War II are known as *gunrei*. *Shōrei* (Ministerial Ordinances) are administrative edicts issued by one or another of the executive ministries (Foreign Affairs, Treasury, etc.)

LOCATING THE TEXT OF A LAW. Diet enactments and executive ordinances are published on their promulgation in the following official sources:

(1) *Kampō.*

(2) *Hōrei zensho.* This is the official compendium of all laws and executive ordinances. Texts are taken from *Kampō*, arranged numerically within each class (Diet Enactments, Cabinet Ordinances, etc.), and published monthly. Its index is similar to that of *Kampō*, and in other respects it may be used in much the same way as the more inclusive publication. In addition, it is the only adequate source for the texts of laws promulgated between 1868 and 1883.

(3) Other current collections of Diet legislation. There are four of these, published by the House of Representatives, the House of Councilors, the Ministry of Justice, and the Supreme Court.[8] These appear to be identical except for pagination.

---

[8] The titles are, respectively, *Kokkai tsūka hōritsu-shū,* · *Kokkai seitei-hō, Kokkai hōritsu-shū,* and *Kokkai hōritsu-shū.* All are postwar publications.

They are not indexed. Hence, they are less convenient to use than *Kampō*. Since they are not recognized as having the same degree of authenticity as *Kampō*, they should be used only when the corresponding issue of *Kampō* is not available.

The arrangement in all these series is first by class (Diet Enactment, Cabinet ordinance, etc.) and within each class chronologically by date of promulgation. Laws and ordinances are numbered chronologically, the numbers starting over again each year. Laws may thus be referred to in the following manner: Imperial Ordinance number 251, 1913; Law number 10, 1949; Cabinet Ordinance number 5, 1957. Each law and ordinance also carries an official title, sometimes lengthy, which may be used for further clarification but need not appear as part of an ordinary bibliographic citation.

Citation of a law or ordinance by number and year makes it possible for a reader to locate the text in short order. When the number is not known, it may be necessary to refer to a subject index. The most voluminous of these is *Hōrei sakuin sōran*,[9] published in 1936. It is worthless for legislation passed since that time, and moreover does not include earlier legislation if it was not in force at the time of compilation. Efficient use necessitates knowledge of the particular subject heads and reference codes which the editor has used, but it is an indispensable tool for students of the subject.

For current legislation, *Hōrei sakuin* and its serial continuation, *Nihon hōrei sakuin*, serve the same purpose. The former indexes laws which were promulgated or amended or became inoperative between December, 1945, and August, 1949.

TEXTS IN ENGLISH. The *Official Gazette*, which was an English-language version of *Kampō* published during the period 1946–52 for the benefit of Allied occupation authorities, includes translations of laws and similar documents promul-

---

[9] Masujima Rokuichirō, ed. (2 vols.; Tokyo, Osaka, 1936).

gated during that time. No publication in English deals as thoroughly with any other period, though there have been two series of selected translations that deserve mention. The *English Version of Japan's Official Gazette*[10] corresponds to issues of *Kampō* from September 1, 1953, to February 16, 1954. It is not as complete as the title would imply. The *EHS Law Bulletin Series—Japanese Laws in English Version*[11] is a current serial publication which includes English translations of important laws.

STATE OF CURRENT LEGISLATION. The foregoing sections have dealt with the problem common in historical research of where to find the text of a particular past legislative enactment or executive decree. We turn now to problems of a different sort—where to learn what the law says now on a particular question, or what it said at some other time in the past. This task is facilitated by the continuous existence since the 1890s of a set of *legal codes*: the civil code, criminal code, code of civil procedure, code of criminal procedure, and commercial code. These five, plus the Constitution, are collectively known as the *Roppō*, literally the "six codes."

The official compendium of laws and orders currently in effect is *Genkō hōrei shūran*.[12] From 1907 until 1930 this came out at (roughly) two-year intervals, with supplements in the intervening years. Since 1930 it has been issued in loose-leaf form, additions and amendments being sent to subscribers as they occur. The arrangement is by subjects. A general table of contents at the beginning is supplemented by a more detailed table at the beginning of each large section. For each law the text indicates by year and number the original legislative enactment and all subsequent amendments to it.

---

[10] International Public News Agency, comp. (2 vols.).
[11] Eibun Hōrei-sha, comp. (loose leaf; Tokyo, current).
[12] Naikaku Shokikan-shitsu kiroku-ka, comp. (Tokyo, from 1907).

The great size of the foregoing work makes it extremely difficult to use. Both specialists and laymen therefore tend to prefer the selective collections known as *Roppō zensho*. Several different series have been issued at various times under this or similar titles. All have been published by commercial houses, and the compilers have been mainly legal scholars at the most prestigious Japanese faculties of jurisprudence. Two current series of this type are put out by the Yūhikaku and Iwanami companies.[13]

Chapter, subchapter, and article numbers were officially assigned to the various parts of the Japanese legal codes when they were first adopted. These remained constant until 1947, when a revised version of the codes with somewhat different structure went into effect. One sometimes finds in scholarly works citations such as "Articles 731–71 of the Civil Code." So long as the time of reference is clear, this is a satisfactory way of referring to the law currently operative on a certain subject. For instance, the above citation, for any date after 1947, would refer to the existing law on marriage and divorce.

THE COURTS AND CASE LAW. The emphasis on codes is one of the principal features which distinguish the Japanese legal system from our own. As in other countries having code law, the texts of codified statutes are accorded primary legal authority. This is not to say, however, that judicial precedents have no place in the Japanese legal system. Lawyers and judges make extensive use of them as guides to the interpretation of written statutes. Case law—the body of written judicial decisions used in this manner—is therefore an important field of the bibliography of Japanese law.

The Japanese Supreme Court (known as Daishin-in until 1947 and Saikō Saiban-sho thereafter) has issued the main

---

[13] Wagatsuma Sakae and Miyazawa Toshiyoshi, ed., *Roppō zensho* (Tokyo, Yūhikaku, current); Suekawa Hiroshi, ed. [*Iwanami*] *Roppō zensho* (Tokyo, current).

series of its own decisions and those of other high courts. These are *Daishin-in hanketsu-roku* (covering 1898–1921), *Daishin-in minji* (or *keiji*) *hanrei-shū*, (1922–47), *Saikō Saiban-sho hanrei-shū* (begun 1948), and *Kōtō Saiban-sho hanrei-shū* (from 1949). Supreme Court decisions from 1875 until the first issuance of the serial collection in 1898 have been published since 1957 as *Meiji zenki Daishin-in minji hanketsu-roku*. Decisions of lower courts have also been published in a number of different series, most of them put out by private agencies. Consult a bibliography of legal materials for details.

COMMENTARIES. Pride of place among a variety of collected commentaries on statutes and codes should go to the current serial *Hōritsu-gaku taikei, kommentāru-hen*.[14] A large number of legal scholars have contributed to this collection, which consists of law texts, each annotated with scholars' and judges' interpretations.

TREATIES. Treaties to which Japan is a signatory are published from time to time in a collection called *Jōyaku isan*.[15] Each set is limited to treaties still operative at the time of publication. Another set, *Kyū jōyaku isan*,[16] brought together the texts of all the treaties which had become inoperative by the time it was published. The texts in these sets are authentic versions, in Japanese as well as in other languages.

The *Jōyaku isan* should not be confused with another collection, *Jōyaku-shū* (since 1922). Here there appear the texts of a great variety of treaties and other international agreements, to which Japan was not necessarily a party but in which Japanese diplomats and authorities might have an interest. Texts are in some or all of the authentic versions, and some treaties are translated into Japanese. These, and the four following

---

[14] The parent series commenced publication in 1950.

[15] Gaimu-shō Jōyaku-kyoku, comp., various editions dated 1900, 1912, 1918, 1925, 1936, etc.

[16] Gaimu-shō Jōyaku-kyoku, comp. (4 vols.; Tokyo, 1930–36).

publications were compiled by the Foreign Ministry (Gaimu-shō Jōyaku-kyoku).

For texts of very recent treaties with Japan as signatory there is a current loose-leaf serial publication, the *Genkō jōyaku shūran*. Newly issued sheets may be inserted as they appear, and treaties removed when they become inoperative.

The best index and guide to treaties in effect up to 1957 is *Jōyaku benran* (published 1958). This contains a chronological list of all treaties between Japan and other countries, with citations of their locations in the sets mentioned above; a list arranged topically by subjects of major concern; and a list arranged by other contracting countries. This publication makes obsolete the similarly organized *Jōyaku mokuroku* (1936), whose terminal date of inclusion is 1934. Since 1955, there has also been an annual index to operative treaties known as *Genkō jōyaku ichiran*, giving the title, date of conclusion, effective date, and citation of official texts for each item.

THE ALLIED OCCUPATION OF JAPAN. The Occupation, which lasted from September, 1945, until April, 1952, did not abolish the government of Japan but made use of it. The office of the Supreme Commander for the Allied Powers (SCAP) issued its directives to the Japanese government, which put them into effect by means of laws and other administrative acts. Consequently the public attestation of ordinary matters of law and administration during the Occupation period continued as before to be a function of the Japanese authorities. In other words, one should go to *Kampō* (or its English equivalent), *Hōrei zensho*, and other official Japanese publications for the authoritative texts of laws and other matters of public record of that time, even though Japan did not then function as a fully sovereign state. However, for the legal acts of the Occupation itself, one must consult the official English-language publications of the office of the Supreme Commander.

SCAP's directives and other memoranda to the government were known as SCAPINs (i.e., SCAP instructions). The best source is *SCAPINs, Supreme Commander for the Allied Powers' Instructions to the Japanese Government, from 4 September 1945 to 8 March 1952 (not Including Administrative Instructions Designated as SCAPIN-A's)*. A separate index was issued by the same agency.[17]

THE INTERNATIONAL MILITARY TRIBUNAL. One other matter of public record from the Occupation period deserves special mention. This is the official *Proceedings* of the Tokyo War Crimes Trial (International Military Tribunal for the Far East) from 1946 to 1948.

The *Proceedings* is but one of the important series emanating from the Tribunal. It consists of the transcripts of the hearings held by the court as a whole, and in addition, of the texts of those documents submitted by defense or prosecution attorneys which the court adjudged to be relevant. The Defense and Prosecution sections which were established under the Tribunal collected many documents which they did not submit to the judges as evidence, and they submitted others which were not accepted for inclusion in the *Proceedings*. In other words, there existed at the time a much larger number of collected materials than were ever issued in a single publication. Nevertheless, the *Proceedings* is the central body of war crimes materials, and it is furthermore the most widely available and best-organized collection to have come out of the Trial.

There are two main guides to its contents. The *Functional Index* in English, by Paul S. Dull and Michael Umemura,[18] is an alphabetical list of subjects showing the page numbers of the official English-language version of the *Proceedings*. The Asahi

---

[17] *Index of Directives to the Japanese Government, SCAPINs 1–2133.*

[18] *The Tokyo Trials: A Functional Index to the Proceedings of the IMTFE* (Ann Arbor, 1957).

Shimbun has brought out a more comprehensive guide,[19] describing day by day the contents of the *Proceedings* with citations to both the English and Japanese versions of the text, and including as well a detailed kana index of subjects.

[19] Mori Kyōzō, ed., *Kyokutō kokusai gunji saiban kiroku mokuroku oyobi sakuin* (Tokyo, 1952). For further information on Tribunal archives see Delmer M. Brown, "Recent Japanese Political and Historical Materials" in *American Political Science Review*, 43 (Oct. 1949), pp. 1010–17; Horwitz, *The Tokyo Trial* (New York, 1950), pp. 576–77.

Appendix I. Technicalities of Style

THE PECULIARITIES of the Japanese language make for a number of technical problems in reporting in English the results of one's research from Japanese sources. Other problems stem from the fact that Japanese scholars have adopted conventions for bibliographic citation and the documentation of sources that are somewhat different from those of the West. In addition, the elementary matter of transcribing Japanese words and sentences into roman letters requires that one learn the rules accepted by scholars and apply them consistently.

Western scholars should adhere wherever possible to the stylistic conventions accepted in the Western academic community. There are many helpful guides to them, of which those mentioned here are personal preferences. *The Modern Researcher* by Jacques Barzun and Henry F. Graff (New York, 1957) offers sound advice on basic principles of research and presentation. *A Manual for Writers of Term Papers, Theses and Dissertations* by Kate L. Turabian (Chicago, 1955) suggests solutions to the mechanical problems encountered in composing footnotes, bibliographies, tables, and charts. This book and the University of Chicago's *Manual of Style*, of which it is a digest, are designed to offer standards for scholarly writing that is to be presented to a publisher or typist. Another guide to technical points of presentation has been issued by the Modern Language Association.[1] "The *Far Eastern Quarterly* Style Sheet"[2] gives

[1] William Riley Parker, "The MLA Style Sheet," *PMLA Publications of the Modern Language Association*, LXVI (April, 1951), pp. 3–27.

[2] *The Far Eastern Quarterly*, XV, No. 2 (February, 1956).

supplementary information useful for scholars in the field of Asian studies.

Conventions of style of the kind laid down in these guides exist for the convenience of scholars, who may deviate from them in those exceptional instances when they are not useful. *A Manual of Style* requires, for example, that the names of the books of the Bible and of all other sacred scriptures are neither underlined nor enclosed in quotation marks. In other words, these books follow a completely different rule from that which applies to ordinary book titles. The rule is good as far as it goes, and scholars and publishers customarily respect it. But how can one apply it to the sacred scriptures of Japanese religions? Is *Kojiki* (*Record of Ancient Matters*) a scripture of the Shinto faith, as modern Shintoists have frequently asserted, or is it merely a work of history? What about the thousands of titles in the ill-defined Buddhist canon? Or *Daigaku Wakumon*, a commentary on the Confucian classic *The Great Learning*? Or *The Great Learning* itself?

There are certain other cases in which students of Japan must make their own rules of style—or, better, adopt the practices current among their colleagues. The following are some pointers on technicalities of citation, punctuation, and the like, for which the style manuals cited above are not entirely helpful.

CITING TITLES OF JAPANESE WORKS. Charles Hamilton, in *Code for Descriptive Cataloging*, suggests the following rule:

> In modern books, a title page or cover equivalent to a title page is usually to be preferred as the source of title. If the title page is chiefly decorative or is absent, as in many older books and facsimile editions, the first page of the main text may be expected to provide the most satisfactory title.[3]

The titles of many modern Japanese works begin with short

---

[3] (Berkeley, 1953), p. 1.

descriptive phrases meaning "new edition," "revised and enlarged," or the like. Note that both scholars and librarians usually ignore these phrases when filing the titles (as in an alphabetical index or bibliography), but are careful to include them enclosed in brackets when they cite the works in full.

NAMES OF JAPANESE PUBLISHING AGENCIES—SHORTENED FORMS. If you decide to identify the publisher of a book in a bibliographic citation, you may wish to use a shortened form (e.g., "Iwanami" instead of "Iwanami Shoten") in accordance with the practice adopted for Western books. If you do so, you should make sure that the shortened form is truly distinctive and meaningful to readers.

DATE OF PUBLICATION. This matter is a morass. Until modern times Japanese bibliographers indicated the date of a book in wholly different ways from those now accepted in the West. Often the only date appearing in a work was that on which the author wrote (or perhaps finished writing) his preface. In the case of a modern Japanese publication, one has the opposite problem of selecting the most meaningful date from the plethora that customarily appear on the colophon. These may include dates of first publication, first printing, publication or printing of the most recent revised edition, or publication or printing of the copy in hand. Copyright dates, as such, are rarely indicated. A numbered "edition" of a book may be identical except for the colophon with some or all of the previous editions. On the other hand, changes of substance or of pagination may appear in a new impression which is not described as a revised edition.

Perhaps there is no convention which adequately meets all of the researcher's needs. In order for him to direct his readers to a copy of a work identical in content and pagination with that which he cites, he must obviously make use of the information which he finds printed in the work itself. The date of publication of the last revision of the book either in substance or in pagination would presumably be the most useful of all, but, as explained above, that date may be unknowable. The safest procedure, and the one which most American libraries and scholars follow, is to choose the latest date that appears on the colophon of the copy used. This will usually be the date on which that copy was printed. If any confusion is likely to arise from your choice of a date, you should indicate exactly what the date means.

> Example: Itō Tasaburō, *Nihon hōken seido-shi* (7th printing, Tokyo, Yoshikawa Kōbunkan, 1958).

As a *reader* of scholarly works in Western languages, you should be aware of the confusions that exist. You should not, for example, assume that a "publication date" in a bibliographic citation is that of first publication. It may be, but again it may not. Still less can be concluded from such a citation as to the date when the book was *written*.

VOLUME NUMBER IN CITATIONS. The English word "volume" is rather tricky, when one stops to think about it. Sometimes it means an individually bound book, but sometimes it does not. Normally, at least, it refers to a single division, containing a whole sequence of page numbers, in a large work. There are several words in Japanese that are roughly comparable, and they are just as troublesome. The important thing to remember is that the function of a volume number in a citation is to identify a single sequence of consecutively numbered pages. The unit which you call "volume two" in a citation may be called *dai nikan, dai nisatsu,* or even *dai nihen* or *dai nibu* in Japanese. The numeral for "two" may not even appear in the Japanese, for the character *ge* 下 has the same meaning in the case of two-volume works, and the character *chū* 中 in the case of three-volume works. However, you must not cite as volume two any unit which is not clearly identified as such *in print* somewhere inside the Japanese original.

Separately bound divisions of some large Japanese books bear no volume numbers at all. Even if the owners of the set which you consult have assigned numbers to them, you must find some other means (subtitles, perhaps, or chapter numbers) of identifying them.

Note that the word *kan* 卷 sometimes means "volume" and at other times (particularly in premodern books) corresponds more closely to a chapter. You should try not to confuse the two meanings. If a chapter (*kan*) of a book carries its own separate pagination, it should take the place of a numbered volume in your citation.

> Example: Rai San'yō, *Nihon gaishi*, chapter 3, p. 5, or:
> Rai San'yō, *Nihon gaishi*, kan 3, p. 5.

CAPITALIZATION IN TITLES. Apply one of the permissible rules for English-language titles[4] as strictly as possible, and be consistent.

WORD DIVISION. The basic rule—put spaces between words —is not very helpful, since even trained linguists sometimes disagree about just what constitutes a Japanese word. Nevertheless, the perplexities of this subject are such that no other easy rule of thumb can be relied upon. The following conventions appear to be preferred among American writers of textbooks and other scholars who have transcribed Japanese phrases and sentences into the Roman alphabet.

1. Postpositional particles (*tenioha*) are treated as whole words.
2. Double particles and multiple particles are treated as though each element were a separate word. (Examples: *ni mo; no ni; made mo; na no de; o ba.*)
3. A verb or adjective, together with all of its inflective or agglutinative endings, is treated as a single word, except where a *tenioha* intervenes. (Examples: *yomimasu; yomaseraremashita; yonde mo ii desu; tabetakunakatta no de arimasu.*)

---

[4] Turabian, *Manual for Writers*, p. 29.

4. A hyphen is used to connect morphemic elements some or
all of which are not full words. (For examples, see the
numerous instances in the present book in which hyphens
have been used in book titles.) It should be noted that some
scholars tend to avoid the use of hyphens, preferring that
a morpheme like *shi* (history), for example, be treated
either as a full word (as in *Dai Nihon shi*) or as an un-
detachable element of a word (as in *Nihon gaishi*).

Librarians use a variety of codes for Japanese word division,
and the American Library Association is considering a unified
code which should apply to book titles and other matters of
interest to them.[5]

ROMANIZATION. Two substantially different systems exist
for the transcription of Japanese into the Roman alphabet, as
well as minor modifications of each of them. The Hepburn
system, or Old Romanization, in one of another of its versions,
is most frequently used among scholars of the English-speaking
world, and is the one to which the lay public as well have
become accustomed, on account of its wide use in newspapers
and through the official standardizations of the Board of
Geographic Names.[6] One modification of the Hepburn system,
that of the 1942 edition of *Kenkyusha's New Japanese-English
Dictionary*, is required in manuscripts submitted to the three
principal American journals of Far Eastern studies.

The other main family of romanization systems, including
the *Nippon-siki* and the *Kokutei-siki*, is preferred by many
scholars on account of its close correspondence to the sound
system of the Japanese language. For example, one version of
the system is used in the textbook of spoken Japanese by
Bernard Bloch and Eleanor Harz Jorden.[7] Since 1937 the

---

[5] *Cataloging Rules of the American Library Association and the Library of Congress:
Additions and Changes 1949–1958* (Washington, 1959).

[6] *Sixth Report of the United States Geographic Board: 1890–1932* (Washington,
1933), pp. 44–45.

[7] *Spoken Japanese* (2 vols.; New York, 1945).

Kokutei-siki has been designated as official or semiofficial by the Japanese government, which, however, continues to permit the use of the Old Romanization in international communications and for place names.[8]

DIACRITICAL MARKS. The only diacritical marks needed for ordinary purposes of romanized transcription are the ones which indicate a lengthened vowel. Conventional systems of romanization use for this purpose either a macron (‾) or a circumflex (^). Though individual publishers may require one or the other of these symbols, the two may be regarded as wholly equivalent. Of course, only one of them should be used in any single article, book, or publication. To this end, you are justified in replacing one of them with the other even when you quote directly a romanized transcription in another work.

CHINESE CHARACTERS IN ENGLISH TEXTS. You may incorporate into your paper or book the equivalents in Japanese writing of transcribed Japanese names, words, or phrases, but note that the Chinese characters do not usually obviate the romanized transcriptions. They should appear directly after the transcription, either enclosed in parentheses or without any intervening punctuation.

If typists or printers balk at mixing roman and Chinese symbols in the same text, they might still be persuaded to make space for a single glossary of Chinese characters at the end of your book or article. Such a glossary is similar to an appendix of "backnotes," as individual names or phrases in it are referred to by means of superscripts within the text. If numerals are used for superscripts to ordinary footnotes or backnotes, another sequence of symbols (usually lower-case letters of the alphabet) must be used to refer to the glossary of characters.

[8] See Kokugo Gakkai, comp., *Kokugo-gaku jiten* (Tokyo, 1955), p. 971.

The Old Romanization, the *Nippon-siki*, and the *Kokutei-siki* are described in Edwin O. Reischauer, "Rōmaji or Rōmazi," *Journal of the American Oriental Society*, LX (1940), pp. 82–89.

NAMES OF PERSONS. In transcribing the names of Japanese, Chinese, and Koreans, it is the almost universal practice of Far Eastern scholars to retain the native order—surnames first. Note the following exceptions:

1. Certain well-known figures of recent times have preferred that their names be transcribed in the Western order, or in other nonstandard ways. (Examples: Joseph Neesima; Daisetz Suzuki; T. V. Soong.) To do otherwise would smack of pedantry, and might even be misleading.

2. Some publishers, particularly of newspapers and magazines, demand that names of persons who lived after a certain date (variously determined by different publishers) be transcribed in the Western order. (Examples: Yoshida Shōin [1830–59]; Shigeru Yoshida [1878–   ]. Yoshida Tōgo [1862–1918] would appear to be a borderline case.)

3. If for any reason a Chinese or Japanese is referred to by a patently occidental given name, baptismal name, or nickname, the personal name should always precede the surname. (Examples: Paul Tsuchihashi, Butch Konoe.)

4. A man's nationality or residence, rather than his birth or ancestry, normally determines whether his name should be written in the Oriental or in the Western manner.

Appendix II. Additional Problems and Solutions

I. Convert the following dates to the Western calendar:

1. 慶長六年九月十五日
2. 寛永二年二月八日
3. 正保三年七月二十日
4. 明暦二年六月十八日
5. 享保十年十一月二十八日

II. Find the date in the Japanese calendar which corresponds to each of the following:

1. December 1, 1393
2. May 1, 1413
3. February 6, 1445
4. November 1, 1468
5. September 1, 1766
6. January 15, 1795
7. March 1, 1800
8. July 20, 1816
9. March 3, 1820
10. April 14, 1833

PROBLEMS MAKING USE OF NEMPYŌ (CHRONOLOGICAL TABLES).

I. Answer the following questions using the appropriate *nempyō*. In each case, find the exact date of the Japanese calendar on which the event described took place.

1. In April, 1854, Yoshida Shōin attempted to stow away to America. Where did the event take place? What was the name of the ship?

2. In February, 1845, a resolution was introduced in the United States Congress regarding commercial relations with Japan. Who introduced the resolution?

3. In August, 1855, the United States government appointed a diplomatic representative to Japan. Who was the official appointed? What was his rank?

4. In June, 1858, Ii Naosuke assumed an important shogunate office. What was the office?

5. In what way did the government take cognizance of Takashima Shūhan's knowledge in a special field in July 1842?

II. What information can be found in historical *nempyō* about the items described below? In the answer, the dates should be converted to the Western calendar.

1. The events in the life of Soga no Emishi on 大化元年六月己酉.

2. The turning point in the career of Sugawara no Michizane which occurred on 延喜元年正月戊申.

3. The new office assumed by Taira Kiyomori on 仁安二年二月庚辰.

4. An event of importance in the history of printing which took place on 寶龜元年四月戊午.

5. The code of ethical maxims drawn up on 推古天皇十二年甲子夏四月戊辰.

PROBLEMS FOR CHAPTER 4

Determine the following information for each of the men given below: romanization of his name; his birth and death dates (as accurately as possible) according to the Western calendar; his claim to fame (in as brief a form as possible; e.g., "president of General Motors," "Confederate general," or "essayist"). In addition, cite by page all biographies of the man which are readily available.

1. 西山拙齋
2. 存應
3. 假名垣魯文
4. 御子左爲明
5. 東ケ崎潔
6. 淡海三船
7. 源經基
8. 源滿仲
9. 龍肅
10. 笠信太郎

PROBLEMS FOR CHAPTER 7

Write a brief description of each of the following works on the basis of the information which can be found in *Kokusho kaidai*, *Gunsho ichiran*, *Shiseki kaidai*, and *Kokushi bunken kaisetsu*. The description should include pertinent facts on authorship, date of writing, character of the work, and its importance. Indicate the name of at least one collection (*sōsho*) in which each work can be found.

1. 梅松論
2. 令集解
3. 語孟字義
4. 本朝文粹
5. 皇代記
6. 李花集
7. 拾芥抄
8. 建武年中行事
9. 釋日本紀
10. 江家次第

PROBLEMS FOR CHAPTER 8

Translate with scholarly annotations the material which you find in the *Koji ruien* relating to each of the following:

1. British castaways in Japan in 1850. Note: the word for castaway is 漂流.
2. 俗言
3. 修文館－横濱
4. 耶蘇敎－經典
5. 出目高

SOLUTIONS TO PROBLEMS FROM CHAPTER 2

I.

1. October 10, 1601 (N.S.)
2. March 16, 1625 (N.S.)
3. August 30, 1646 (N.S.)
4. August 8, 1656 (N.S.)
5. January 1, 1726 (N.S.)

II.

1. Meitoku 4, 10th month, 27th day
2. Ōei 20, 4th month, 2nd day
3. Bunnan 1, 12th month, 30th day
4. Ōnin 2, 10th month, 17th day
5. Meiwa 3, 7th month, 27th day
6. Kansei 6, 11th intercalary month, 25th day
7. Kansei 12, 2nd month, 6th day
8. Bunka 13, 6th month, 26th day
9. Bunsei 3, 1st month, 19th day
10. Tempō 4, 2nd month, 25th day

SOLUTIONS TO PROBLEMS ON NEMPYŌ

I. The answers for questions 1–5 can be found in the *Nihon gaikō nempyō narabi-ni shiyō bunsho* compiled by the *Gaimu-shō* (Tokyo, 1955) vol. I.

II. Problems 1–5 may be answered by reference to one or more of the following:

Hioki Shōichi, ed., *Bunka dai nempyō* (Tokyo, 1955–56)
Kuroita Katsumi, ed., [*Kōtei*] *Kokushi kenkyū nempyō* (Tokyo, 1939)

Hioki Shōichi, ed., *Kokushi dai nempyo* (6 vols.; Tokyo, 1935).

The dates in the Western calendar for each problem are as follows:

1. July 11, 645 (O.S.)
2. February 16, 901 (O.S.)
3. March 4, 1167 (O.S.)
4. May 25, 770 (O.S.). The event is described as having occurred on another date in the same year in the *Kokushi dai nempyō*.
5. May 6, 604 (O.S.)

SOLUTIONS TO PROBLEMS FOR CHAPTER 4

Questions 1–10 may be answered by consulting one or more of the following works:

> *Dai Nihon jimmei jisho*
> *Dai hyakka jiten*
> *Dai jimmei jiten*
> Seki Giichirō and Seki Yoshinao, eds., *Kinsei kangaku-sha denki dai jiten* (Tokyo, 1943)
> *Kugyō bunin*
> *Dai Nihon shi*, Vols. IV–VIII, Index volume.
> *Nihon keifu sōran*
> *Bunka jimmei-roku*
> *Jinji kōshin-roku*
> *Zen Nihon shinshi-roku*
> *Taishū jinji-roku*
> *Seishi kakei dai jiten*
> Hioki Shōichi, ed., *Nihon rekishi jimmei jiten* (Tokyo, 1938)
> Heibon-sha Gendai Nihon Jimmei Jiten Henshū-bu, *Gendai Nihon jimmei jiten* (Tokyo, 1955).

The readings for the names are as follows:

1. Nishiyama Sessai
2. Zon'ō
3. Kanagaki Robun

4. Mikohidari Tameaki
5. Tōgasaki Kiyoshi
6. Ōmi Mifune
7. Minamoto Tsunemoto
8. Minamoto Mitsunaka. Note that in the biography in the *Dai Nihon shi* (V, 378–80) the birth date of Mitsunaka, son of Tsunemoto, is given as the year 912/13, five years earlier than that of his father, who is said to have been born in 917/18 (*Dai Nihon shi*, V, 349–50).
9. Ryō Susumu
10. Ryū Shintarō

SOLUTIONS TO PROBLEMS FOR CHAPTER 7

The readings generally agreed upon for these titles are as follows:

1. *Baishō-ron.*
2. *Ryō no shūge* or *Ryō shūge*. The *Gunsho ichiran* calls it the *Ryō no shikkai.*
3. *Go-mō jigi.*
4. *Honchō monzui.*
5. *Kōdai-ki.*
6. *Rika-shū.*
7. *Shūkai-shō.*
8. *Kemmu nenjū gyōji.*
9. *Shaku Nihon-gi.*
10. *Gōke shidai. Kokusho kaidai* renders the name as *Kōke shidai.*

SOLUTIONS TO PROBLEMS FOR CHAPTER 8

I. By using the subject index in Volume LX of the *Koji ruien* the material to be translated may be located in the following places:

1. XXVIII, 525–26.
2. XLV, 832.
3. XXXVIII, 1045–46.

4. XXXVI, 1134. In this case, the index refers only to the entire section on *Yasokyō* (XXXVI, 1099–1295) and the entries along the upper margin must be used to locate the subsection for *keiten*.
5. XXII, 121–22.

Bibliography

I. WORKS IN WESTERN LANGUAGES

The American Historical Association's Guide to Historical Literature. New York, Macmillan, 1961.

Bandō Shōjun, Hanayama Shōyū, Satō Ryōjun, Sayeki Shinkō, and Shima Keiryū, eds. *A Bibliography on Japanese Buddhism.* Tokyo, CIIB Press, 1958.

Barzun, Jacques, and Henry F. Graff. *The Modern Researcher.* New York, Harcourt, Brace and Company, 1957.

Bibliographical List of Japanese Learned Journals: Humanities and Social Sciences. Comp. by Ministry of Education, Bureau of Higher Education and Science. Tokyo, published by compiler, 1959.

Bloch, Bernard, and Eleanor Harz Jorden. *Spoken Japanese.* 2 vols. New York, Henry Holt, 1945.

Borton, Hugh, Serge Elisséeff, William W. Lockwood, and John C. Pelzel, comps. *A Selected List of Books and Articles on Japan.* Cambridge, Harvard–Yenching Institute, 1954.

BPR: American Book Publishing Record. Philadelphia, R. R. Bowker Company, monthly, from 1960.

Bramsen, William. *Japanese Chronological Tables.* Tokyo, Seishi Bunsha, 1880.

Brinkley, F. *An Unabridged Japanese-English Dictionary.* Tokyo, Sanseidō, 1896.

Brown, Delmer M. "Recent Japanese Political and Historical Materials," in *American Political Science Review,* 43 (October, 1949).

Cataloging Rules of the American Library Association and the Library of Congress 1949–1958. Washington, Library of Congress, 1959.

Columbia University Masters' Essays and Doctoral Dissertations on Asia, 1875–1956. Comp. by the East Asiatic Library, Columbia University. New York, published by compiler, 1957.

Dazai Osamu. *The Setting Sun.* Tr. by Donald Keene. Norfolk, Conn., J. Laughlin, 1956.

Dissertation Abstracts, A Guide to Dissertations and Monographs Available in Microform. Ann Arbor, University Microfilms, from 1938.

Doctoral Dissertations Accepted by American Universities. New York, H. W. Wilson, 1934–1955.

Dull, Paul S., and Michael Umemura. *The Tokyo Trials, A Functional Index to the Proceedings of the International Military Tribunal for the Far East.* Ann Arbor, University of Michigan Press, 1957. (University of Michigan, Center for Japanese Studies, Occasional Papers, no. 6).

EHS Law Bulletin Series, Japanese Laws in English Version. Comp. by Eibun Hōrei-sha. 8 vols., loose leaf. Tokyo, published by compiler, current.

English Version of Japan's Official Gazette. Comp. by International Public News Agency. 2 vols. Tokyo, published by compiler, 1953–1954.

External Research: A List of Recently Completed Studies. Lists *East Asia.* Comp. by U.S. Department of State, Office of Intelligence Research and Analysis. (These are published annually in October.)

External Research: A List of Studies Currently in Progress. Lists *Japan.* Comp. by U.S. Department of State, Office of Intelligence Research and Analysis. (These are published annually in April.)

"The *Far Eastern Quarterly* Style Sheet." *The Far Eastern Quarterly,* vol. xv (2 February 1956).

Garde, P. K. *Directory of Reference Works Published in Asia.* Paris, UNESCO, 1956.

Gardner, Charles S. *Chinese Traditional Historiography.* Cambridge, Harvard University Press, 1938.

Gillis, Irvin Van Gorder, and Pai Ping-ch'i. *Japanese Personal Names.* Peking, Hwa Hsing Press, 1940.

——— *Japanese Surnames.* Peking, Hwa Hsing Press, 1939.

Hall, John W. *Japanese History, A Guide to Japanese Reference and Research Materials.* Ann Arbor, University of Michigan Press, 1954.

Hall, Robert B., and Toshio Noh. *Japanese Geography, A Guide to Japanese Reference and Research Materials.* Ann Arbor, University of Michigan Press, 1956.

Hamilton, Charles E. *Code for Descriptive Cataloging.* Berkeley, University of California General Library, 1953.

Han Yu-shan. *Elements of Chinese Historiography.* Hollywood, Calif., W. M. Hawley, 1955.

The Harvard Guide to American History. Cambridge, Harvard University Press, 1954.

Horwitz, Solis. *The Tokyo Trial.* New York, Carnegie Endowment for International Peace, 1950. (*International Conciliation,* no. 465, November, 1950).

Index to American Doctoral Dissertations. Ann Arbor, University Microfilms, from 1957.

An Index to Japanese Law, 1867–1961. (Preliminary draft of a complete bibliography of all books, pamphlets, articles, essays, statutes, cases, and other legal materials concerning Japanese law in the English language. Conference on Japanese Law, Harvard Law School, September, 1961). Mimeographed.

Index Translationum, International Bibliography of Translations. Paris, International Institute of Intellectual Cooperation, 1932–1940, nos. 10–31; new series: Paris, UNESCO, from 1949.

International Index, A Quarterly Guide to Periodical Literature in the

Social Sciences and Humanities. New York, H. W. Wilson, from 1907.

International Military Tribunal for the Far East. *Proceedings.* Tokyo, published by compiler, 1946–1948.

K.B.S. Bibliography of Standard Reference Books for Japanese Studies. Vol. 1: Generalia. Tokyo, Kokusai Bunka Shinkokai, 1959.

Kenkyusha's New Japanese-English Dictionary. Ed. by Takenobu Yoshitaro. American Edition: Cambridge, Harvard University Press, 1942.

———— Ed. by Senkichiro Katsumata. Tokyo, Kenkyusha, 1954.

List of Japanese Government Publications in European Languages 1945–1955. Tokyo, National Diet Library, 1956.

A Manual of Style. 11th ed. Chicago, University of Chicago Press, 1949.

"The MLA Style Sheet." Comp. by William Riley Parker. *PMLA*, vol. LXVI (April, 1951), 3–27.

Morley, James. "Check List of Seized Japanese Records in the National Archives," in *The Far Eastern Quarterly*, vol. IX (3 May 1950).

Nelson, Andrew Nathaniel. *The Modern Reader's Japanese-English Character Dictionary.* Rutland, Vermont, Charles E. Tuttle, 1962.

New York Times Index. New York, New York Times, from 1913.

Official Gazette (English Edition). Tokyo, Government Printing Agency, 1946–1952.

Praesent, Hans. *Bibliographie von Japan, 1938–1943.* (Unpublished photostats of cards.)

Reader's Guide to Periodical Literature. New York, H. W. Wilson, from 1905.

Reischauer, Edwin O., "Rōmaji or Rōmazi," in *Journal of the American Oriental Society*, vol. 60 (1940).

Remer, Charles F., and Saburo Kawai. *Japanese Economics,*

A Guide to Japanese Reference and Research Materials. Ann Arbor, University of Michigan Press, 1956. (University of Michigan, Center for Japanese Studies, Bibliographical Series, no. 5).

Rose-Innes, Arthur. *Beginners' Dictionary of Chinese-Japanese Characters.* New 4th ed. Tokyo, Meiseisha Publishing Company, 1960.

Sixth Report of the United States Geographic Board, 1890–1932. Washington, United States Government Printing Office, 1933.

Soothill, William Edward, and Lewis Hodous. *A Dictionary of Buddhist Terms.* London, Kegan Paul, Trench, Trubner and Co., Ltd., 1937.

Stucki, Curtis W. *American Doctoral Dissertations on Asia, 1933–1962, Including Appendix of Master's Theses at Cornell University.* Ithaca, New York, 1963. (Cornell University, Department of Asian Studies, Data Paper, no. 50).

Supreme Commander for the Allied Powers. *SCAPINs, Supreme Commander for the Allied Powers' Instructions to the Japanese Government, from 4 September 1945 to 8 March 1952 (not Including Administrative Instructions Designated as SCAPIN-A's).* Tokyo, published by compiler, 1952.

——— *Index of Directives to the Japanese Government, SCAPINs 1-2133.* Tokyo, published by compiler, 1950.

Tanizaki, Jun'ichirō. *The Makioka Sisters.* Tr. by Edward G. Seidensticker. New York, Alfred A. Knopf, 1957.

Tsuchihashi, Paul Yachita. *Japanese Chronological Tables.* Tokyo, Sophia University Press, 1952.

Turabian, Kate L. *A Manual for Writers of Term Papers, Theses and Dissertations.* Chicago, University of Chicago Press, 1955.

Uyehara, Cecil H. "Checklist of Archives in the Japanese Ministry of Foreign Affairs, Tokyo, Japan, 1868–1945." Washington, Library of Congress, 1954.

Uyehara, Cecil H. *Leftwing Social Movements in Japan*. Tokyo, Rutland, Vt., Charles E. Tuttle, 1959.

Waley, Arthur, tr. *The Tale of Genji* by Lady Murasaki. New York, The Modern Library, 1960.

Ward, Robert E., and Hajime Watanabe. *Japanese Political Science, A Guide to Japanese Reference and Research Materials*. Revised ed. Ann Arbor, University of Michigan Press, 1961. (University of Michigan, Center for Japanese Studies, Bibliographical Series, no. 1).

Wenckstern, Friedrich von. *A Bibliography of the Japanese Empire, 1859–93*. Leiden, Brill, 1895.

Winchell, Constance H. *Guide to Reference Books*. Chicago, American Library Association, 1951. First Supplement: 1954. Second Supplement: 1956. Third Supplement: 1960.

Yamagiwa, Joseph K. *Japanese Language Studies in the Shōwa Period, A Guide to Japanese Reference and Research Materials*. Ann Arbor, University of Michigan Press, 1961. (University of Michigan, Center for Japanese Studies, Bibliographical Series, no. 9).

Young, John. *Checklist of Microfilm Reproductions of Selected Archives of the Japanese Army, Navy, and Other Government Agencies, 1868–1945*. Washington, Georgetown University Press, 1959.

II. WORKS IN JAPANESE

(A list of some important works of traditional Japanese history may be found in the text, on pages 95–101.)

Amano Keitarō 天野敬太郎. [*Hompō*] *shoshi no shoshi* [本邦] 書誌の書誌. Tokyo, Mamiya Shōten, 1933.

Asahi Nenkan 朝日年鑑. From 1924. Osaka, Asahi Shimbun-sha, from 1923.

Bakumatsu Meiji shimbun zenshū 幕末明治新聞全集. Comp. by Meiji Bunka Kenkyū-kai 明治文化研究會. Ed. by Osatake Takeki 尾佐竹猛. Tokyo, Taisei-dō, 1934–1935.

[*Oda*] *Bukkyō dai jiten* [織田]佛教大辭典. Ed. by Oda Tokunō 織田得能. Enlarged, revised edition. Tokyo, Ōkura Shuppan K. K., 1954.

[*Mochizuki*] *Bukkyō dai jiten* [望月]佛教大辭典. Ed. by Mochizuki Shinkō 望月信亨. Rev. by Tsukamoto Zenryū 塚本善隆. Tokyo, Seikai Seiten Kankō Kyōkai, 1955–1958. 8 vols.

Bunka dai nempyō 文化大年表. Comp. by Hioki Shōichi 日置昌一. Vols. 1–2, 5–6. Tokyo, Ōkura Shuppan K. K., 1955–1956. 4 vols. published to date.

Bunka jimmei-roku 文化人名錄. Comp. by Nihon Chosaku-ken Kyōgi-kai 日本著作権協議會. Tokyo, published by compiler, from 1951.

Bussho kaisetsu dai jiten 佛書解說大辭典. Comp. by Ono Gemmyō 小野玄妙. Tokyo, Daitō Shuppan-sha, 1933–1936. 12 vols.

Chikamatsu goi 近松語彙. Comp. by Ueda Mannen 上田萬年 and Higuchi Yoshichiyo 樋口慶千代. Tokyo, Fuzambō, 1930.

Chōsa kikan tosho-kan sōran 調査機関図書館総覧. Comp. by Semmon Tosho-kan Kyōgi-kai 専門図書館協議会. Tokyo, published by compiler, 1956.

Dai bukan 大武鑑. Comp. by Hashimoto Hiroshi 橋本博. Tokyo, Daikō-sha, 1935–1936. 12 vols.

Dai genkai 大言海. Comp. by Ōtsuki Fumihiko 大槻文彦. Tokyo, Fuzambō, 1932–1937. 5 vols.

Dai hyakka jiten 大百科事典. Tokyo, Heibon-sha, 1931–1935. 28 vols.

[*Shinsen*] *Dai jimmei jiten* [新撰] 大人名辭典. Tokyo, Heibon-sha, 1937–1941. 9 vols.

Dai jimmei jiten 大人名事典. Tokyo, Heibon-sha, 1953–1955. 10 vols.

Dai jiten 大辭典. Tokyo, Heibon-sha, 1934–1935. 26 vols.

Dai jiten 大字典. Comp. by Ueda Mannen 上田萬年. Tokyo, Keisei-sha, 1940.

Dai Kan-Wa jiten 大漢和辞典. Comp. by Morohashi Tetsuji 諸橋轍次. Tokyo, Taishū-kan Shoten, 1955–1960. 13 vols.

Dai Nihon chimei jisho 大日本地名辭書. Comp. by Yoshida Tōgo 吉田東伍. Tokyo, Fuzambō, 1911–1913. 7 vols.

Dai Nihon dokushi chizu 大日本讀史地圖. Comp. by Yoshida Tōgo 吉田東伍. Tokyo, Fuzambō, 1939.

Dai Nihon Ishin shiryō 大日本維新史料. Comp. by Tōkyō Daigaku Shiryō Hensan-jo 東京大學史料編纂所. Tokyo, published by compiler, from 1938.

[*Shintei-ban*] *Dai Nihon jimmei jisho* [新訂版] 大日本人名辭書. Comp. by Dai Nihon Jimmei Jisho Kankō-kai 大日本人名辭書刊行會. Tokyo, published by compiler, 1937. 5 vols.

Dai Nihon kahei shi 大日本貨幣史. Comp. by Yoshida Kensuke 吉田賢輔. Ed. by Honjō Eijirō 本庄榮治郎. Tokyo, Chōyō-kai, 1925–1926. 8 vols.

Dai Nihon kinsei shiryō 大日本近世史料. Comp. by Tōkyō Daigaku Shiryō Hensan-jo 東京大學史料編纂所. Tokyo, published by compiler, from 1953.

[*Shūtei*] *Dai Nihon kokugo jiten* [修訂] 大日本國語辭典. Comp. by Ueda Mannen 上田萬年 and Matsui Kanji 松井簡治. 12th printing. Tokyo, Fuzambō, 1958.

Dai Nihon ko-monjo 大日本古文書. Comp. by Tōkyō Daigaku Shiryō Hensan-jo 東京大學史料編纂所. Tokyo, published by compiler, from 1901.

Dai Nihon shi 大日本史. Tokyo, Dai Nihon Yūben-kai, 1928–1929. 16 vols.

Dai Nihon shiryō 大日本史料. Comp. by Tōkyō Daigaku Shiryō Hensan-jo 東京大學史料編纂所. Tokyo, published by compiler, from 1901.

Dai Nihon Teikoku Gikai-shi 大日本帝國議會史. Comp. by Dai Nihon Teikoku Gikai-shi Kankō-kai 大日本帝國議會史刊行會 Tokyo, Shizuoka, published by compiler, 1926–1930. 18 vols.

Dai Nihon Teikoku tōkei nenkan 大日本帝國統計年鑑. Comp.

by Naikaku Tōkei-kyoku 內閣統計局. Tokyo, published by compiler, 1882–1941.

Daishin-in keiji hanketsu-roku 大審院刑事判決錄. Comp. by Daishin-in 大審院. Tokyo, published by compiler, 1896–1921.

Daishin-in keiji hanrei-shū 大審院刑事判例集. Comp. by Daishin-in 大審院. Tokyo, Hōsō-sha, 1922–1947.

Daishin-in minji hanketsu-roku 大審院民事判決錄. Comp. by Daishin-in 大審院. Tokyo, published by compiler, 1894–1921.

Daishin-in minji hanrei-shū 大審院民事判例集. Comp. by Daishin-in 大審院. Tokyo, Hōsō-kai, 1922–1946.

Dokushi biyō 讀史備要. Comp. by Tōkyō Teikoku Daigaku Shiryō Hensan-jo 東京帝國大學史料編纂所. Tokyo, Naigai Shoseki K. K., 1933.

Gaimu-shō kōhyō-shū 外務省公表集. Comp. by Gaimu-shō Jōhō Bunka-kyoku Hōdō-ka 外務省情報文化局報道課. Tokyo, published by compiler, from 1922.

Gendai kazoku fuyō 現代華族譜要. Tokyo, Nihon Shiseki Kyōkai, 1929.

Gengo dai jiten 諺語大辭典. Comp. by Fujii Otoo 藤井乙男. Tokyo, Yūhō-dō, 1926.

Genji monogatari jiten 源氏物語辭典. Comp. by Kitayama Keita 北山谿太. Tokyo, Heibon-sha, 1957.

Genji monogatari taisei 源氏物語大成. Comp. by Ikeda Kikan 池田龜鑑. Tokyo, Chūō Kōron-sha, 1953–1956. 8 vols.

Genkō hōrei shūran 現行法令輯覽. Comp. by Naikaku Shokikan-shitsu Kiroku-ka 內閣書記官室記錄課. Tokyo, Teikoku Chihō Gyōsei Gakkai, from 1907.

Genkō jōyaku ichiran 現行条約一覽. Comp. by Gaimu-shō Jōyaku-kyoku 外務省条約局. Tokyo, published by compiler, from 1957.

Genkō jōyaku shūran 現行条約集覽. Comp. by Gaimu-shō Jōyaku-kyoku 外務省条約局. Tokyo, published by compiler, from 1956.

[*Sanshō*] *Gunsho ichiran* [参照] 群書一覽. Comp. by Ozaki Masayoshi 尾崎雅嘉. Ed. by Irita Seizō 入田整三. Tokyo, Nichiyō Shobō, 1931.

Zoku gunsho ichiran 續群書一覽. Comp. by Nishimura Kanebumi 西村兼文. Ed. by Irita Seizō 入田整三. Tokyo, Nichiyō Shobō, 1926.

Gunsho kaidai 群書解題. Comp. by Zoku Gunsho Ruijū Kansei-kai 續群書類從完成會. Tokyo, published by compiler, from 1961.

[*Shinkō*] *Gunsho ruijū* [新校] 羣書類從. Comp. by Hanawa Hokiichi 塙保巳一. Ed. by Ueda Mannen 上田萬年 and others. Tokyo, Naigai Shoseki K. K., 1928–1932. 21 vols.

Gunsho sakuin 羣書索引. Comp. by Mozume Takami 物集高見. Tokyo, Kōbun-ko Kankō-kai, 1928. 3 vols.

Hatano Ken'ichi 波多野賢一 and Yayoshi Mitsunaga 彌吉光長. [*Kenkyū chōsa*] *sankō bunken sōran* [研究調査] 参考文献總覽. Tokyo, Asahi Shobō, 1934.

Hisho ruisan 秘書類纂. Ed. by Itō Hirobumi 伊藤博文. Rev. by Hiratsuka Atsushi 平塚篤. Tokyo, Hisho Ruisan Kankō-kai, 1933–1936. 27 vols.

Hon'yaku bungaku mokuroku 翻訳文学目錄. Comp. by Kokuritsu Kokkai Tosho-kan 国立国会図書館. Tokyo, Kazama Shobō, 1959.

Hōrei sakuin 法令索引. Comp. by Kokuritsu Kokkai Tosho-kan Chōsa Rippō Kōsa-kyoku 国立国会図書館調査立法考査局. Tokyo, published by compiler, 1949.

Hōrei sakuin sōran 法令索引總覽. Ed. by Masujima Rokuichirō 増島六一郎. Tokyo and Osaka, Yukawa Kōbun-sha, 1936. 2 vols.

Hōrei zensho 法令全書. Tokyo, Naikaku Insatsu-kyoku, from 1885.

Hōritsu-gaku taikei 法律學体系. *Kommentāru-hen* コンメンター ル篇. Tokyo, Nihon Hyōron Shinsha, from 1951.

Bibliography

Ishin nisshi 維新日誌. Ed. by Hashimoto Hiroshi 橋本博. Tokyo, Shizuoka Kyōdo Kenkyū-kai, 1932–1935. 20 vols.

Ishin shi 維新史. Comp. by Ishin Shiryō Hensan Jimu-kyoku 維新史料編纂事務局. Tokyo, Meiji Shoin 1941–1943.

Jinji kōshin-roku 人事興信錄. Tokyo, Jinji Kōshin-jo, from 1903.

Jōyaku benran 条約便覧. Comp. by Gaimu-shō Jōyaku-kyoku 外務省条約局. Tokyo, published by compiler, 1958.

Jōyaku isan 條約彙纂. Comp. by Gaimu-shō Jōyaku-kyoku 外務省條約局. Tokyo, published by compiler, from 1925.

Jōyaku mokuroku 條約目錄. Comp. by Nihon Gakujutsu Shinkō-kai 日本學術振興會. Tokyo, published by compiler, 1936.

Jōyaku shū 条約集. Comp. by Gaimu-shō Jōyaku-kyoku 外務省条約局. Tokyo, published by compiler, from 1922.

Kampō 官報. Comp. by Naikaku Insatsu-kyoku 內閣印刷局. Tokyo, published by compiler, from 1883.

Kanchō kankō tosho geppō 官廳刊行圖書月報. Tokyo, Naikaku Insatsu-kyoku, 1938–1943.

Kanchō kankō tosho mokuroku 官廳刊行圖書目錄. Tokyo, Naikaku Insatsu-kyoku 1927–1937.

Kanchō kankō-butsu sōgō mokuroku 官庁刊行物総合目録. Comp. by Kokuritsu Kokkai Tosho-kan 国立国会図書館. Tokyo, published by compiler, from 1952.

Kansei chōshū sho-kafu 寛政重脩諸家譜. Comp. by Yashiro Hirokata 屋代弘賢 and others. Ed. by Hotta Masaatsu 堀田正敦. Tokyo, Eishin-sha Shuppan-bu, 1917–1918. 8 vols.

Kanseki kaidai 漢籍解題. Comp. by Katsura Koson 桂湖邨. Tokyo, Meiji Shoin, 1922.

[*Kadokawa*] *Kan-Wa chū jiten* [角川] 漢和中辞典. Comp. by Kaizuka Shigeki 貝塚茂樹, Fujino Iwatomo 藤野岩友, and Ono Shinobu 小野忍. Tokyo, Kadokawa Shoten, 1959.

Kawase Kazuma 川瀬一馬. *Nihon shoshi-gaku no kenkyū* 日本書誌學之研究. Tokyo, Dai Nihon Yūben-kai, 1943.

Keizai-shi bunken 經濟史文献. Ed. by Honjō Eijirō 本庄榮治郎. Tokyo, Nihon Hyōron Shinsha, from 1957.

Keizai-shi nenkan 經濟史年鑑. Ed. by Honjō Eijirō 本庄榮治郎 and others of the Keizai-shi Kenkyū-kai 經濟史研究會. Tokyo, Nihon Hyōron Shinsha, 1955–1956.

Kindai bungaku kenkyū sōsho 近代文学研究叢書. Comp. by Shōwa Joshi Daigaku Kindai Bungaku Kenkyū-shitsu 昭和女子大学近代文学研究室. Tokyo, Shōwa Joshi Daigaku Kōyō-kai, from 1956.

Kō-bunko 廣文庫. Comp. by Mozume Takami 物集高見. Tokyo, Kō-bunko-kai, 1916. 20 vols.

Koji ruien 古事類苑. Comp. by Hosokawa Junjirō 細川潤次郎 et al. Tokyo, Koji Ruien Kankō-kai, 1931–1936. 60 vols.

Kokinshū sō-sakuin 古今集総索引. Comp. by Nishishita Kyōichi 西下經一 and Takizawa Sadao 滝沢貞夫. Tokyo, Meiji Shoin, 1958.

Kokka taikan 國歌大觀. Comp. by Matsushita Daisaburō 松下大三郎 and Watanabe Fumio 渡邊文雄. Tokyo, Chūbun-kan Shoten, 1931. 2 vols.

Zoku kokka taikan 續國歌大觀. Comp. by Matsushita Daisaburō 松下大三郎. Tokyo, Chūbun-kan Shoten, 1931. 2 vols.

Kokugo-gaku jiten 国語学辞典. Comp. by Kokugo Gakkai 国語学会. Tokyo, Tōkyō-dō, 1955.

Kokushi bunken kaisetsu 國史文獻解說. Comp. by Endō Motoo 遠藤元男 and Shimomura Fujio 下村富士男. Tokyo, Asakura Shoten, 1957.

Kokushi dai nempyō 國史大年表. Comp. by Hioki Shōichi 日置昌一. Tokyo, Heibon-sha, 1935. 6 vols.

[Shintei zōho] kokushi taikei [新訂増補] 國史大系. Ed. by Kuroita Katsumi 黑板勝美. Tokyo, Kokushi Taikei Kankō-kai, from 1935.

[Zōtei] kokusho kaidai [増訂] 國書解題. Comp. by Samura Hachirō 佐村八郎. Tokyo, Rokugō-kan, 1926. 2 vols.

Bibliography

Kōtō Saiban-sho hanrei-shū 高等裁判所判例集. Comp. by Saikō Saiban-sho 最高裁判所. Tokyo, published by compiler, from 1949.

[*Nihon dai jiten*] *Kotoba no izumi* [日本大辭典] 言泉. Comp. by Ochiai Naobumi 落合直文. Tokyo, Ōkura Shoten, 1929. 6 vols.

Kugyō bunin 公卿補任. Ed. by Kuroita Katsumi 黑仮勝美. Tokyo, Kokushi Taikei Kankō-kai, 1934–1938. 5 vols.

Kurita Motoji 栗田元次. *Sōgō kokushi kenkyū* 綜合國史研究. Tokyo, Dōbun Shoin, 1935. 3 vols.

Kuroita Katsumi 黑板勝美. *Kokushi no kenkyū* 國史の研究. Tokyo, Iwanami Shoten, 3rd rev. ed., 1931. 3 vols.

Kyokutō kokusai gunji saiban kiroku mokuroku oyobi sakuin 極東国際軍事裁判記録目録及び索引. Ed. by Mori Kyōzō 森恭三. Tokyo, Asahi Shimbun, 1952.

Kyōsan-shugi jiten, 共產主義辞典 "*Pocket Dictionary of Communism.*" Comp. by Hosokawa Karoku 細川嘉六 and Kawakami Kan'ichi 川上貫一. Tokyo, Nisshin Shoten, 1949.

Kyū jōyaku isan 舊條約彙纂. Comp. by Gaimu-shō Jōyaku-kyoku 外務省條約局. Tokyo, published by compiler, from 1934.

Man'yō-shū taisei 萬葉集大成. Comp. by Shimonaka Yasaburō 下中彌三郎. Tokyo, Heibon-sha, 1953–1956. 22 vols.

Meiji bunka zenshū 明治文化全集. Comp. by Yoshino Sakuzō 吉野作造. Tokyo, Nihon Hyōron-sha, 1928–1930. 24 vols.

Meiji Taishō kokusei sōran 明治大正國勢總覽. Tokyo, Tōyō Keizai Shimpō-sha, 1929.

Meiji Taishō zaisei shōran 明治大正財政詳覽. Tokyo, Tōyō Keizai Shimpō-sha, 1929.

Meiji zenki Daishin-in minji hanketsu-roku 明治前期大審院民事判決録. Tokyo, Sanwa Shobō, from 1957.

Morimoto Kakuzō 森本角藏. *Nihon nengō taikan* 日本年號大觀. Tokyo, Meguro Shoten, 1933.

Nihon bijutsu jiten 日本美術辞典. By Noma Seiroku 野間淸六 and Tani Nobukazu 谷信一. Tokyo, Tōkyō-dō, 1952.

[*Zōho kaitei*] *Nihon bungaku dai jiten* [增補改訂] 日本文學大辭典. Comp. by Fujimura Tsukuru 藤村作. Tokyo, Shinchō-sha, 1951–1952. 8 vols.

Nihon chimei dai jiten 日本地名大辭典. Comp. by Sawada Hisao 澤田久雄. Tokyo, Nihon Shobō, 1939. 6 vols.

Nihon chimei hatsuon jiten 日本地名発音辞典. Comp. by Nihon Hōsō Kyōkai 日本放送協会. Tokyo, Nihon Hōsō Shuppan Kyōkai, from 1959.

Nihon chimei jiten 日本地名事典. Comp. by Watanabe Akira 渡辺光. Tokyo, Asakura Shoten, 1954–1955. 4 vols.

Nihon gaikō bunsho 日本外交文書. Comp. by Gaimu-shō 外務省. Tokyo, Nihon Kokusai Rengō Kyōkai, from 1936.

Nihon gaikō bunsho, Kindai in-yō-reki taishō-hyō 日本外交文書·近代陰陽曆對照表. Comp. by Gaimu-shō 外務省. Tokyo, published by compiler, 1951.

Nihon gaikō nempyō narabi ni shuyō bunsho 日本外交年表竝主要文書. Comp. by Gaimu-shō 外務省. Tokyo, Nihon Kokusai Rengō Kyōkai, 1955. 2 vols.

Nihon hōrei sakuin 日本法令索引. Comp. by Kokuritsu Kokkai Tosho-kan Chōsa Rippō Kōsa-kyoku 国立国会図書館調査立法考査局. Tokyo, published by compiler, from 1951.

[*Sakoku jidai*] *Nihonjin no kaigai chishiki* [鎖國時代] 日本人の海外知識. Comp. by Kaikoku Hyakunen Kinen Bunka Jigyō-kai 開國百年記念文化事業會. Tokyo, Kangen-sha, 1953.

Nihon keifu sōran 日本系譜綜覽. Comp. by Hioki Shōichi 日置昌一. Tokyo, Kaizō-sha, 1936.

[*Kaihan*] *Nihon keizai-shi bunken* [改版] 日本經濟史文献. Ed. by Honjō Eijirō 本庄榮治郎. Tokyo, Nihon Hyōron-sha, 1933.

Nihon keizai-shi dai-san bunken 日本經濟史第三文献. Ed. by Honjō Eijirō 本庄榮治郎, Yoshikawa Hidezō 吉川秀造, and Matsuyoshi Sadao 松好貞夫. Tokyo, Nihon Hyōron Shinsha, 1953.

Nihon keizai-shi shin bunken 日本經濟史新文献. Ed. by Honjō Eijirō 本庄榮治郎. Tokyo, Nihon Hyōron-sha, 1942.

Nihon keizai tōkei-shū 日本経済統計集. Comp. by Nihon Tōkei Kenkyū-jo 日本統計研究所. Tokyo, Nihon Hyōron Shinsha, 1958.

Nihon kokusei jiten 日本國政事典. Comp. by Nihon Kokusei Jiten Kankō-kai 日本國政事典刊行會. Tokyo, Rengō Shuppan-sha, from 1953.

Nihon koten bungaku taikei 日本古典文學大系. Tokyo, Iwanami Shoten, from 1957.

Nihon no sankō tosho 日本の参考図書. Comp. by Nihon no Sankō Tosho Henshū Iinkai 日本の参考図書編集委員会. Tokyo, published by compiler, 1962.

Nihon rekishi chizu 日本歴史地図. Comp. by Nishioka Toranosuke 西岡虎之助 and Hattori Shisō 服部之総. Tokyo, Zenkoku Kyōiku Tosho K. K., 1956.

Nihon rekishi dai jiten 日本歴史大辞典. Comp. by Kawade Takao 河出孝雄. Tokyo, Kawade Shobō, 1956–1960. 20 vols.

Nihon shakai minzoku jiten 日本社会民俗辞典. Comp. by Nihon Minzoku-gaku Kyōkai 日本民族学協会. Tokyo, Seibun-dō Shinkō-sha, 1954–1960. 4 vols.

[*Kaitei zōho*] *Nihon-shi jiten* [改訂増補] 日本史辞典. Comp. by Kyōto Daigaku Bungaku-bu Kokushi Kenkyū-shitsu 京都大学文学部国史研究室. Tokyo, Sōgen-sha, 1960.

Nihon Shiseki Kyōkai sōsho 日本史籍協會叢書. Ed. by Hayakawa Junzaburō 早川純三郎, Iwasaki Hideshige 岩崎英重, Ōtsuka Takematsu 大塚武松, etc. Tokyo, Nihon Shiseki Kyōkai, 1915–1931. 188 vols.

Nihon shokuin-roku 日本職員録. Comp. by Jinji Kōshin-jo 人事興信所. Tokyo, published by compiler, from 1947.

[*Zōtei*] *Nihon sōsho sakuin* [増訂] 日本叢書索引. Comp. by Hirose Bin 廣瀬敏. Tokyo, Kazama Shobō, 1957.

Nihon tōkei nenkan 日本統計年鑑 ("Japan Statistical Year Book"). Ed. by Sōrifu Tōkei-kyoku 総理府統計局. Tokyo, Nihon Tōkei Kyōkai (Japan Statistical Association), from 1950.

Nihon tōkei sō-sakuin 日本統計総索引. Comp. by Semmon Tosho-kan Kyōgi-kai 専門図書館協議会. Tokyo, Tōyō Keizai Shimpō-sha, 1959.

Nihon tosho-kan sōran 日本圖書館總覽. Comp. by Nihon Gakujutsu Kaigi 日本學術會議. Tokyo, Shizen-ryō Gakusho Kyōkai, 1954.

Rekishi-gaku no seika to kadai 歴史學の成果と課題. Ed. by Rekishi-gaku Kenkyū-kai 歴史學研究會. Tokyo, Iwanami Shoten, from 1950.

Roppō zensho 六法全書. Ed. by Wagatsuma Sakae 我妻栄 and Miyazawa Toshiyoshi 宮沢俊義. Tokyo, Yūhikaku, current.

[Iwanami] Roppō zensho [岩波] 六法全書. Ed. by Suekawa Hiroshi 末川博. Tokyo, Iwanami Shoten, current.

Saikō Saiban-sho hanrei-shū 最高裁判所判例集. Comp. by Saikō Saiban-sho 最高裁判所. Tokyo, published by compiler, from 1948.

Sankō tosho no kaidai 参考圖書の解題. By Yayoshi Mitsunaga 彌吉光長. Tokyo, Risō-sha, 1955.

Sankō tosho sōgō mokuroku 参考図書総合目録. Comp. by Kokuritsu Kokkai Tosho-kan 国立国會図書館. Tokyo, published by compiler, 1955.

Sansei sōran 三正綜覽. Comp. by Naimu-shō Chiri-kyoku 内務省地理局. Tokyo, Teito Shuppan-sha, 1932.

Seishi kakei dai jiten 姓氏家系大辭典. Comp. by Ōta Akira 太田亮. Supervised by Ueda Mannen 上田萬年 and Mikami Sanji 三上參次. Tokyo, Seishi Kakei Dai Jiten Kankō-kai, 1934–1936. 3 vols.

Sekai dai hyakka jiten 世界大百科事典. Tokyo, Heibon-sha, 1959. 32 vols.

Sengo hōgaku bunken sō-mokuroku 戦後法学文献総目録. Ed. by Hōritsu Jihō Henshū-bu 法律時報編集部. Tokyo, Nihon Hyōron Shinsha, 1954–1955. 2 vols.

Shakudo sōkō 尺度綜考. By Fujita Motoharu 藤田元春. Tokyo, Tōkō Shoin, 1929.

Shigaku zasshi sō-mokuroku 史学雑誌総目錄. Comp. by Shigakkai 史学会. Tokyo, Yamakawa Shuppan-sha, 1952.

Shimbun shūsei Meiji hennen-shi 新聞集成明治編年史. Comp. by Shimbun Shūsei Meiji Hennen-shi Hensan-kai 新聞集成明治編年史編纂會. Ed. by Nakayama Yasumasa 中山泰昌. Tokyo, Zaisei Keizai Gakkai, 1935–1940. 15 vols.

Shirin sō-mokuroku 史林総目錄. Comp. by Shirin 史林. Kyoto, Shigaku Kenkyū-kai, 1958.

Shirin sōmoku sakuin 史林總目索引. Comp. by Shirin 史林. Kyoto, Naigai Shuppan Insatsu K. K., 1935.

[*Tōkyō Daigaku*] *Shiryō Hensan-jo tosho mokuroku* [東京大學] 史料編纂所圖書目錄. Comp. by Shiryō Hensan-jo 史料編纂所. Tokyo, Tōkyō Daigaku Shuppan-kai, from 1955.

Shiryō sōran 史料綜覽. Comp. by Tōkyō Teikoku Daigaku Bungaku-bu Shiryō Hensan-gakari 東京帝國大學文學部史料編纂掛. Tokyo, Chōyō-kai, from 1925. 22 vols.

Shiseki kaidai 史籍解題. Comp. by Endō Motoo 遠藤元男, etc. Tokyo, Heibon-sha, 1936.

Shokuin-roku 職員錄. Tokyo, Ōkura-shō Insatsu-kyoku, from 1886.

Shōwa hōbō sō-mokuroku 昭和法寶總目錄. Ed. by Takakusu Junjirō 高楠順次郎 and Watanabe Kaigyoku 渡邊海旭. Tokyo, Taishō Issai-kyō Kankō-kai, 1929–1934. 3 vols.

Shuppan nenkan 出版年鑑. Tokyo, Shuppan Nyūsu-sha, from 1951.

Sōgō Nihon minzoku goi 綜合日本民俗語彙. Comp. by Minzoku-gaku Kenkyū-jo 民俗學研究所. Tokyo, Heibon-sha, 1955–1956. 5 vols.

Taishō shinshū Daizōkyō 大正新修大藏經. Rev. and ed. by Takakusu Junjirō 高楠順次郎 and Watanabe Kaigyoku 渡邊海旭. Tokyo, Taishō Issai-kyō Kankō-kai, 1914–1932. 85 vols.

Taishū jinji-roku 大衆人事錄. Tokyo, Teikoku Himitsu Tantei-sha, from 1925.

Tōkei chōsa gaido bukku 統計調査ガイドブック. By Masaki
    Chifuyu 正木千冬 and Matsukawa Shichirō 松川七郎.
    Tokyo, Tōyō Keizai Shimpō-sha, 1951.

[*Kaitei-ban*] *Tōyō kanji jiten* [改訂版] 当用漢字辞典. Comp. by
    Seki Kan'ichi 関宦市 and Tomiyama Tamizō 富山民蔵.
    Tokyo, Chūkyō Shuppan K. K., 1961.

Yamaguchi Ryūji 山口隆二. *Nihon no tokei* 日本の時計.
    Tokyo, Nihon Hyōron-sha, 1950.

Zasshi kiji sakuin, jimbun kagaku hen 雑誌記事索引・人文科学編.
    Comp. by Kokuritsu Kokkai Tosho-kan 国立国会図書館.
    Tokyo, Kinokuniya Shoten, from 1949.

Zasshi kiji sakuin, shizen kagaku hen 雑誌記事索引・自然科学編.
    Comp. by Kokuritsu Kokkai Tosho-kan 国立国会図書館.
    Tokyo, Kinokuniya Shoten, from 1950.

Zen-Nihon shinshi-roku 全日本紳士錄. Comp. by Jinji Kōshin-jo
    人事興信所. Tokyo, published by compiler, from 1950.

Zen-Nihon shuppan-butsu sō-mokuroku 全日本出版物総目録.
    Comp. by Kokuritsu Kokkai Tosho-kan 国立国会図書館.
    Tokyo, published by compiler, from 1951.

[*Kokuritsu Kokkai Tosho-kan*] *Zōsho mokuroku* [国立国会図書館]
    蔵書目録. Tokyo, Kokuritsu Kokkai Tosho-kan, from 1960.

Index

Index